The Art of Selling the Family Business

THE ART OF SELLING THE FAMILY BUSINESS

RESPONSIBLE STEWARDSHIP OF FAMILY WEALTH

Jonathan Pellegrin

Foreword by
John A. Davis

Cambridge Institute for Family Enterprise
Boston, Massachusetts

ISBN-13: 9781546460138
ISBN-10: 1546460136

Cover design by Vickey Hanson Williams
Library of Congress Control Number: 2017910192
CreateSpace Independent Publishing Platform
North Charleston, South Carolina

To the three smartest and wisest women I know,
Patricia Mellencamp, Amy Pellegrin, and Dae Mellencamp

CONTENTS

Avoiding the Three-Generation Rule

S ince the start of the field of family business in the mid-1980s, academics and consultants have largely focused on how the actions and attitudes of the family, the family ownership group, and the leaders and employees of the business influence the performance and survival of the family business. This orientation emphasizing the support and continuity of the family business is obvious in the academic journal and magazine articles in the field. The name for the field, after all, is family business. We didn't call it the business family field. But maybe we should have.

The emphasis on supporting the family business was a natural way to start the field and has generated useful findings. But this focus is also limiting. It seems to imply that a family should try to keep its family business going and in the family's control. Most business families, themselves, have this attitude. In fact, most seem to regard the sale of their healthy business as not just the failure of the business but also as a sign of family failure. Jonathan Pellegrin will cure you of that misconception.

For almost twenty of the nearly forty years I have spent as an academic and an advisor in this field, I, too, was largely focused on understanding long-term family company success. But then my focus shifted to the success and survival of the family. I came to see that we academics and advisors should be most focused on studying and helping business families to survive as economically productive and socially responsible groups. And business families should understand that to be their goal too. Jonathan Pellegrin called that one correctly long before I reached that conclusion.

Like most of my life learnings and shifts in orientation, I needed to be convinced by the data. And I was. If you observe family companies that survive generations, you will see that over time the industries these companies participate in change considerably, often abruptly, and sometimes the industries just go away. Some family companies have the resources, talent, and interest to stay in the game as an industry changes and matures. Company size, relative size (compared to competitors), a strong balance sheet, and an innovative company culture, all backed by a persistent and loyal family ownership group, help a family company weather industry change and disruption. But there are far more losers than winners when industries change, and you have to know if you have what it takes to stay in the game and to prosper. Most families are slow in making this call; most overestimate their ability to compete well in the new environment, and some are delusional.

At the root of much of this poor decision making is the noble attachment families have to their companies. Most families in business strongly prefer to stay in the industry game they know and to keep the company they have grown to love and are identified with. It's not easy but certainly easier to exit a particular industry if the family company has more than one line of business and participates in other industries as well. Then the family can exit a particular business where they can't win and stay in other businesses where they can compete, and their overall company can go on. For family companies that are focused on one line of business, the decision to exit an industry is usually excruciating because it usually means that the whole family company would go away. Their identity as caretakers of this jewel, their image in the community, and the welfare of people they care about are all threatened.

Timely sales of companies are also compromised by opposing interests in the family ownership group. One could choose to mediate these conflicting interests, but most families choose not to.

If a family truly loses interest in the family company, it is emotionally easier to sell it. But very often a loss of interest in the company is accompanied by a lack of attention to it and the industry that it's in. If an industry is changing rapidly, or if the family has not been persistent in reinvesting in its company, when the family is motivated to sell the company, there might be very little value in it.

These dynamics all play out in the movement of family wealth over generations. We all recognize the so-called Three-Generation Rule, expressed in many ways in different languages, that a family that becomes wealthy will lose its wealth in three generations. I have studied "family wealth paths" for over a decade to test the above rule. According to my research, the Three-Generation Rule captures the experience of about 70 percent of all families. Some families lost their wealth faster than three generations. And some—perhaps 15 percent of all families—regenerate their wealth beyond the third generation. If you want to be on the Regeneration Path, you will follow this prescription.

Recognize that businesses come and go, and you must shift the lines of business you are invested in if you want your overall family company to survive, or if you want to survive as a business family. The more successful families I have studied shifted from businesses that were declining (or they didn't have the resources, talent, or interest to continue them) to businesses that had growth potential and were a better fit for the family. Sometimes families who stayed successful financially would sell their entire family company altogether and reemerge in another company. Especially in today's environment of quickly changing industries and shifting interests in families, you need to be prepared to sell at least one of your businesses, if not your entire family company. Pellegrin's book will tell you how to do this.

What you do with the capital you earn by selling your family business also matters in many ways. Families who maintain their financial success mostly invest their capital together (as opposed to dividing it up among the owners to invest separately); they invest in business activities they understand, and they grow family talent to guide and improve their new business activities. Ultimately, they stay a family in business with a different kind of business.

Some people feel this advice—focusing on the growth of family wealth—encourages business families to be too financially oriented and not loyal enough to the work of the family. In response, I would try to persuade you that you can't do good work of any kind without the financial resources or assets to support those activities. You also can't keep families united and loyal to whatever the family builds without sufficient financial resources to motivate the family owners. You simply must keep a wealth perspective if you are going to sustain the good work you want to do.

But I would add the following: creating anything of lasting value involves being passionate about and attached to whatever you are building. You simply won't invest the time, energy, and creativity into something if you are not attached to it.

I admit there is more than a touch of irony in my advice. But here is how you resolve this understanding of value creation: Attach to and nurture activities that deserve your attention and that will grow and return adequate rewards for your efforts. Then be able to detach from these same activities when you can no longer warrant your good efforts. If you own a family business, there will come a time when you need to let it go. This book by Jonathan Pellegrin will explain how you do that.

John A. Davis
Martha's Vineyard
February 25, 2017

PREFACE

Why I Wrote This Book

Over 95 percent of all businesses in the United States and throughout the world are started by a pioneer founder—an independent craftsman and an entrepreneur. Those who succeed can continue flourishing if the founder begins a legacy of passing the baton of leadership and ownership from generation to generation in a timely way.

But multiyear survival is more complicated than just executing a successful succession plan. Today, more than ever, all companies are operating in intensely unforgiving business and competitive environments. In addition, legacy issues that define family companies can make it nearly impossible to muster the agility or the courage to make the difficult decisions critical for survival and effective stewardship of family assets. Examples of family business weaknesses include reluctance to abandon unprofitable product lines and terminate long-standing, loyal employees who are no longer up to the job.

At these critical crossroads, the leaders of businesses must make a decision about the future of the business. There are few options:

- Lead the company through change.
- Pass the baton of leadership to the next generation of the family or to a competent nonfamily executive.
- Procrastinate and do nothing.
- Bring in a partner or merge.
- Sell the company.

These choices have important ramifications. And this book explores informed decision making about selling.

My own experience as a second-generation CEO and owner of the company founded by my father formed the basis of my decade-long research on this topic. After successfully leading and growing our company for eighteen years, I made the decision to sell it. This decision, one of the most difficult of my life, was influenced by the failures of once-successful companies I had witnessed that lost their way and ultimately their value. These tragedies rendered a verdict to me that selling a family company was *not* in itself a sign of a failure—*losing a fortune was.* Passion is a critical fuel of success, and as I realized in my own case, when the passion was dying, it was time to sell.

So, at age forty-nine, I sold our family company, resulting in a very successful harvest. I set up trusts for members of my family, including my unborn grandchildren, and journeyed to Switzerland and the international business school, IMD, where I became an executive in residence. I loved teaching, which is a bit like sales presentations for thought; the students reported that they loved my classes. But with the other faculty, my lack of a doctorate—the proper credential in academia where experience, paradoxically, counts for little—made my on-the-job knowledge less in their eyes. Therefore, I decided to get a doctorate. And I did. In 2000, at the beginning of the new millennium, I returned to the States with a big black-bound book, my dissertation—a tome filled with footnotes, graphs, charts, and interviews with business families throughout Europe and the Americas. It included an index of virtually every essay and book written about family companies. Whew! I will make a few changes and turn this into a book, so I thought. Eighteen years later, I am still wrangling with this fat stack of research.

Why has this taken me so long? Why is it still unfinished? It's not writer's block; I actually like to write almost as much as I enjoy thinking about and talking about business. It's not laziness. When I am focused on a project, I am relentless until the conclusion. It's not fear that no one will read it, or others will think my ideas lame—the ideas and advice I offer here are well tested. I think I finally have the answer: something was out of whack with publishing a long book, with lots of research for family business owners to read when they are in, most likely, a state of indecision, or anxiety, or fear (if they are honest) about the future of their company, to say nothing about the future well-being of generations of their family. After all, my dissertation proved the truth and wisdom of what I learned during the entire process of selling my family company; my experiential knowledge, from boots on the ground, was at the heart of my discoveries.

Well, then what? I decided to share what I learned in the process of selling my company and others selling theirs, extracting the golden nuggets from this experience, in a series of essays that represent a lifetime of learning.

Some of my essays will overlap, because some of my ideas bear repeating. But all the essays are quite short and can be read on the train or over morning coffee.

My e-mail address is jgpellegrin@gmail.com if you need more support, ideas, or information. I have witnessed firsthand the erosion of wealth that can come with a botched sale. Through my consulting, I have gained empathy for the arduousness of this decision and process—rarely talked about in the news other than at the point of sale. (Also, not talked about because "real men" or "strong women" are not supposed to have fear and anxiety and suffer from indecision.)

I know that if you adhere to the principles in these essays, you will protect and be poised to guard your wealth, your legacy, and, as important, your contentment.

Regarding the latter, I have included an essay on aftereffects—on what comes after the money wire hits your bank—during the period following your company's sale. I am trusting that you will have read the previous essays, had a successful sale, that your phone has stopped ringing or texting, and you are wondering "Now what?" Real wisdom does take a lifetime. What an incredible journey!

San Jose del Cabo
March 1, 2017

INTRODUCTION

D uring my career in publishing business magazines, I witnessed far too many times the tragedy of the demise, bankruptcy, and liquidation of once successful and respected companies owned by influential entrepreneurs and respected business families. Pondering those truly sad stories, I always wondered what really happened in those cases and why the owners didn't sell their companies when they had the opportunity, rather than presiding over the burial of a once valuable asset.

I never wanted our family to lose its *successful and respected company*. Our business family story started with my paternal grandfather—a prominent industrial designer, who successfully developed and patented my grandmother's idea to put a light in her refrigerator. His enhancement has been incorporated into every refrigerator since. My grandfather bought a farm for my dad who was studying agriculture in college. Dad brought the same creativity to farming, and his inventiveness led him on the path to becoming a serial entrepreneur. Ultimately the farm and his certified seed business went through several iterations and finally morphed into developing an innovative publishing concept to deliver financial management information to farmers. The magazine served a critical need, as farming was becoming more capital intensive and farmers needed useful education about financial management. It provided a solid, scalable foundation for our family company that over nearly forty years of family ownership developed more than thirty specialized business magazines.

Before joining the family business, I spent two years working for a radio and television broadcasting company and a year with a large retail company in New York. My dad and I subsequently worked together for eight years before I became president and CEO of our Wisconsin-based company. The first six years I worked for my dad was an incredibly positive experience; then our relationship began to deteriorate. As I gained more experience and demonstrated success in the business, my dad and I began to have differences over strategy issues and the direction of the company. In 1975 and 1976, I led trade missions through several African nations for the US Department of Commerce, resulting in an opportunity for me to become a White House Fellow and work in Washington, DC, for the secretary of commerce. I made the decision to leave our family company. When I informed my dad of my plan, he realized I was serious and had a viable alternative. Rather than see me leave, my dad made the decision to turn the leadership of our company over to me (he was fifty-seven; I was thirty-two), and he moved to Hawaii where he developed another successful publishing company with my older brother.

I was so excited about having the opportunity to lead the company. For two years, I had been thinking about what I would do if I were in charge (frustration growing because the date for my ultimate elevation had been so elusive), and now I had my chance. I dug in with such exuberance that both time and balance in my life virtually disappeared. My day at the office began between 4:00 and 5:00 a.m., and I went back after dinner and stayed until I was ready to drop with exhaustion—a routine that continued through the weekends.

During the first four months of my reign, the company was literally deconstructed and put back together according to my vision and beliefs. I sold or closed unprofitable, low potential segments of the business, revamped our production operations, established metrics for every process, changed the organization structure, and identified clear objectives for each manager.

Together with our key people, we developed a plan for growth, which included carefully defining our products and specifically targeting our customers. It worked—the growth of our company exploded—doubling revenue and quadrupling earnings in just three years. To effectively cover our North American market—with editors annually visiting more than six hundred farms and our salespeople visiting thousands of dealers and distributors—our fleet of company airplanes grew to four. Our visibility and reputation also grew, and opportunities seemed to be dropping in our lap. It was an exhilarating time, and our company of young tigers was on the roll.

After spending twenty-six years in this adrenaline-pumping, creative business and eighteen years as CEO, an unexpected surge of excitement surfaced when my twenty-two-year-old daughter, Amy, joined our summer internship program and worked at our company after she received her undergraduate degree. Our employees (members of our extended business family) celebrated the potential emergence of the third generation of Pellegrin family leadership in our company. But her interests and passion took her on another course.

While I loved the excitement, the competition, and the platform our company provided in both business and social communities, I felt like I was losing energy for the business. The extraordinary passion I once had seemed to be fading. I was also profoundly aware of being responsible for our most valuable family asset. Markets and business performance have volatility, and the fluctuations can be severe and even fatal. In fact, product life cycles are ever shorter, and new technology and innovations can blindside businesses and completely change the game—destroying the value of particular businesses. The potential threat of economic losses imposed on our magazines through electronic dissemination of business information worried me. (It was 1993; my worries were a decade early.) I had experienced euphoric highs and abrupt downdrafts in our company—the latter of which produced an increasing amount of fear and anxiety with each occurrence. In retrospect, I was getting scared about potential threats that could erode the value of the company my dad founded and I built—together with a team of talented colleagues.

Even though we were on a five-year run of increasing revenue and profit and the business appeared to be taking on characteristics of a secure annuity, my gut was telling me that it was time for change. When I finally realized that I was no longer as excited about more of the same and I was able to acknowledge that no euphoria of more success would ever offset the despair I would feel about any diminution of value under my watch, I knew it was time. The decision to pursue the sale of our family-owned company was made in the fall of 1993, and the deal was closed on August 1, 1994.

As I've reflected on my thinking about the possibility of selling and subsequently making and carrying out the decision, I've realized the key determinants in my decision were rooted in my dying passion for the business and lack of family interest—combined with increasing fear and anxiety about the potential for disruptive change in my industry, ownership issues, and my stewardship responsibilities. In fact, when the intensity of my fear and anxiety was palpably stronger than the intensity of my passion to continue, making the decision to sell became easier. These personal realizations formed the hypotheses for my study. They have been reinforced time and again in my research with business families who have successfully sold their companies. In addition, business family members who have shared their deep regret for not having sold their companies when the valuations were high and their passion was dying had enormous impact on me.

This book combines scholarship and experience—of others and my own—to present a template for the development and harvest of businesses created with the passion and uniquely crafted cultures found in entrepreneurial and family enterprises. I have purposely used the word "harvest" to illuminate my core message, which comes from my childhood years spent on our family farm in Illinois.

We harvested our crops every year, and finally my father and grandfather "harvested" or sold the farm. The underlying theme in this book suggests that *every* entrepreneurial and family-owned company needs to be harvested or sold in some fashion by the owners. First, mortality dictates that ownership evolves and shareholders change over time. Second, when there are no family successors or wealth creators to competently lead the business or become responsible owners of the business, it should be sold to owners who are both competent and committed to sustaining the success of the business, and the selling families should be monetized for the value of their equity in the company.

In the case of generational ownership transfers within families, it has become my deeply held conviction that succeeding owners must make an "investment," both financial and philosophical, in order to demonstrate their commitment, interest, and worthiness to carry on the ownership of the firm.

I believe that in cases of generational succession, the seniors' financial security should be assured. Succeeding generation members need to assume the risk inherent in carrying on the enterprise as their predecessors did. This involves both proper shareholder education *and* assumption of financial risk to acquire ownership from retiring stockholders. These are critical steps for successors to take not only for the benefit of their predecessors but also for themselves. Family shareholders who have no interest, appetite, or affinity for being responsible owners of the business should be bought out—their shares should be redeemed by the company or purchased by other interested shareholders or family members. When there are no actively interested and capable family successor-owners, it is very wise for the business families to embark on a harvesting strategy for their companies.

It is crucial for enlightened entrepreneurs and family business owners to be ever mindful of the natural order of things, including stages of life, the aging process, health, and mortality, as well as the myriad of the other factors affecting the business, the family, and the owners. Ultimately, for each generation, separation from ownership and leadership of the business is a given. In earlier years, for some family members, separation can also be a gift. Therefore, prudent and continual "harvest" planning is an imperative for all business owners. Successfully selling a family business *is an art*, filled with subtlety and nuances. And that's what this book is about.

CHAPTER 1

SELLING YOUR FAMILY BUSINESS ISN'T NORMAL (ENOUGH)

T he ownership composition of every business changes over time; if nothing else, mortality dictates it. Even if the shares of the company are owned in a trust, beneficiaries change over generations. Therefore, in the interest of truly responsible stewardship, family business owners should monitor at regular intervals their continued ownership of what is typically their largest single asset. A plan should be in place for the careful evaluation of selling if and when circumstances make it the wisest decision for protecting the wealth of the family at any given time.

Family businesses generally evolve over time from the craft of the founder to an enterprise that has value beyond the physical assets of the company. The litmus test for building true value of a company is the extent to which it can be operated successfully without any involvement of the founder. A business that operates simply as the craft of the owner/manager is difficult to sell as an ongoing business at a high price. Of course, the physical assets and the customer lists can be sold, but without the craftsman, there is little intangible value or goodwill that can be leveraged in a sale.

It's often the second generation who begin discovering and capitalizing on the scalable opportunities in the business. There are "wealth builders" in both the family and management who are able to increase the enterprise value beyond the market prices of physical assets.

It's never too early to examine the evolution of a business system and the context in which it exists. The examples that follow—successful companies that reached the third generation and beyond—can serve as templates for families to consider their own situations and become more responsible stewards of their family assets. Successful family companies have wealth creators in each generation. When growth stalls or stops, it is a sign that value is at its peak.

In 1996 when I was an executive-in-residence at IMD in Lausanne, Switzerland, I created, along with Tom Bata (chairman and CEO of Bata Shoe Corporation), the IMD Distinguished Family Business Award (now known as the IMD—Lombard Odier Global Family Business Award). The businesses of all the recipients grew out of the crafts of the founders. However, their sustainable success grew out of new product development, exploiting new markets, acquisitions, and shedding obsolete products, processes, and divisions. Wealth creators drove these initiatives in each generation.

- The Lego Group was founded in 1932 in the carpentry workshop of Ole Kirk Christiansen, in Billund, Denmark. After his shop burned down, he began making miniature models of product ideas, and the miniatures triggered an idea to make toys. Over the years, the products evolved to include the famous interlocking Lego bricks that fueled the explosive growth of the company.
- Thierry Hermès first established Hermès in 1837 as a harness workshop on the Grands Boulevards quarter of Paris dedicated to purveying to European noblemen. He created the finest wrought harnesses and bridles for the carriage trade. Over time the business expanded to include fine saddles and then leather bags to carry the saddles. Subsequent development of fine women's handbags and the famous Hermès silk scarves and ties created the foundation for this fashion giant.
- Puig Beauty and Fashion Group was founded in 1914 by Antonio Puig. As a young man, Puig traveled to France from his home in Barcelona. He was overwhelmed by the assortment of perfumes and beauty products that he saw in Paris and immediately realized that nothing of the sort was available in Spain. The spark for his business idea was ignited. He decided

to become an importer for foreign cosmetics and perfumes. The products would fill a void in Spain. As his business grew, he began to realize his vulnerability to the power of his suppliers, and he began working to develop his own fragrances in order to fully control his source of supply. The products Antonio created achieved market acceptance—helped by having his distribution channel in place. The business then advanced with its own products and subsequently with the products of companies the Puig family acquired as they prospered. Brands include Nina Ricci, Carolina Herrera, Paco Rabanne, Jean Paul Gaultier, Penhaligon's, L'Artisan Parfumeur, Agua Brava, Quorum, Brummel, Victorio & Lucchino, Sportman, Anouk, Azur, and others.

- Fritz Henkel founded the Henkel Group in 1876 in Aachen, Germany. He was a young merchant selling household products and had a passionate interest in science. As a consequence, he amused himself doing research on his products, experimenting with different ingredients and formulations to achieve greater effectiveness. His successful efforts in his makeshift laboratory resulted in the creation of products with demonstrable competitive advantages. This, combined with his knowledge of retail distribution, provided a solid foundation for repeating the process over and over again and growing the company into a global leader in the household products category.

- Ermenegildo Zegna was just twenty years old when he took over his family's small wool-producing business in Trivero, Italy, in 1910. This region had long been an important center for Italy's fabrics and wool industry. Rather than continue as just another "Mom and Pop" wool producer in an Italian village, Zegna decided to narrow the focus of his nascent business and target the men's luxury suit market that was dominated by British wool makers and tailors. Zegna set out to emulate his English counterparts while upping the ante in his quest for quality. Zegna himself traveled around the world in search of the finest wool herds. After establishing his company as *the* producer of the finest wool for men's suits through wedding new technologies with traditional handcrafting techniques, it was a small step for the next generation to begin exploring the actual production of finished goods—made-to-measure and manufactured top of line, expensive men's suits.

- Samuel Curtis Johnson, the original entrepreneur, sold parquet floors in a hardware store during his early working years. In 1886, he acquired the parquet flooring product line and had his independence as a business owner. Recognizing people's need to treat wooden floors, Johnson developed a floor wax that he mixed in a bathtub. It wasn't long before the tail was wagging the dog. Sales of the floor wax outstripped young Sam Johnson's personal sales of parquet floors.

  Under the leadership of his son, grandson, and great-grandson, S. C. Johnson & Sons' business went from a small wax company to four major global enterprises that include household goods, innovative commercial products and services, environmentally responsible polymers, diverse financial services, and some of the most recognized brands in the recreational industry. H. F. Johnson, the third leader of the Johnson family business, adopted a philosophy called "Product Plus" that has surely had a powerful influence on the company's enduring success. Every new Johnson product had to have a distinct advantage over everything else on the market, or it had to be new and unique enough to outstrip the competition.

The common denominators of all these family companies included:

- ability to find the golden nugget—the product or service the market needed and wanted at that time, coupled with the capability to provide it profitably and to make the business scalable;
- commitment to quality that lived up to the family's name;
- discipline to stay focused on their sustainable core business activity while building a rock-solid, defendable foundation before becoming diverted with other unrelated business ideas;

- pride in the products and services they sold, passion for their businesses, confidence to compete effectively, and achieve leadership positions in their market niches;
- ability to profitably grow through adding new products and new geography and getting rid of unprofitable products and unproductive people; and
- a wealth creator in each generation to lead and guide their growth.

These well-known companies have made it through several generations, and their stories cloud reality. Statistics on business failure rates are daunting as the following graph illustrates. According to US government figures, 50 percent of all new business start-ups fail within five years. Getting it right is not easy!

Companies missing the aforementioned characteristics may be better off selling their companies and diversifying and redeploying their assets to protect their wealth for the current and future generations.

Operating a business is not only about generating and raising capital, attracting competent people, developing and producing products and services, getting and keeping customers, and generating revenue that adequately exceeds expenses. It's also about cash flow and liquidity in the short term and over the long haul. Businesses that lose money for protracted periods of time and burn up their equity are sure to fail; there are many cases of profitable companies that became insolvent and failed because they simply ran out of cash. Perhaps they grew too fast and outstripped their equity base and borrowing capacity to finance the business. A common cause of failure is too much focus on the income statement and not enough focus on managing the balance sheet and cash flow—for example, letting accounts receivable and inventory get out of control. Or maybe they were poor managers who didn't know how to operate a profitable business. Businesses that survive ten years or more, let alone those that continue on for generations, are among a truly elite group. They have beaten the tremendous odds of business failure rates.

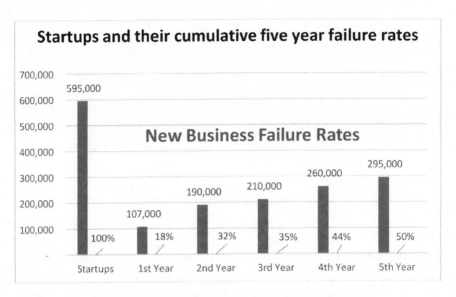

Source: US Bureau of Labor Statistics, April 28, 2016

Necessity is often the mother of invention in many start-up businesses. For example, the founder may have lost his or her job, can't find another, and is forced to earn a living doing the only thing he or she knows how to do. But this time around he or she pulls together the requisite resources him- or herself rather than working for an employer. He or she starts out as an "entrepreneur of one," selling his or her time and talent as a service or through the products he or she makes. A limitation may be the inability or lack of interest in making the business scalable. Achievement of financial targets is not the primary driver in these ventures. Rather, survival—making a living—and the execution and delivery of the craft *to get and keep customers* are primary objectives. Strong and passionate identification with the business, the products, the customers, and the employees—if there are any—underscore the attachment that owner-managers and families have to their enterprises. After all, these businesses are really extensions of the family.

A vital measure of business sustainability is whether or not it can successfully survive beyond the leadership of the founder who is usually a controlling owner-manager. Figures bandied about for several years indicate that only 30 percent of all family-owned companies make it to the end of the second generation; less than 20 percent make it to the end of the third; and fewer than 10 percent make it to the end of the fourth. These numbers have been debunked. They are not right. Too many factors, like successfully selling family companies and reinvesting in new businesses, invalidate past studies of generational mortality. Name changes, mergers, and reconfiguration of family ownership also skew the figures.

In spite of the historical mortality numbers and the fact that it is difficult for families to preside over generational ownership and management transitions, there are numerous factors that cloud accurate measurement of family business continuity. Among all the business reasons that can affect family business mortality rates, in my opinion, *the biggest obstacle in generational transfers between the first and second generations is the reluctance of the founder to let go and pass the leadership baton to the next generation*. This reticence of family business leaders to step aside when it's time to pass the baton affects successful succession efforts among the other ownership constellations—siblings and cousins—as well.

Founders generally are better doers than teachers and have difficulty in effectively grooming successors. Other reasons contributing to the so-called high mortality rates include lack of competence and interest among succeeding generation members to either successfully carry on the leadership and management of the businesses or become responsible, contributing owners and stewards of the family businesses through active and constructive involvement in ownership and governance structures.

Family Business Models

Family-owned and owner-managed companies have very different characteristics from investor-owned corporations. The latter have been the focus of study and research for years by academics at leading colleges and universities. Entrepreneurship and family businesses are still relatively new fields of discipline and are still struggling to achieve parity in academia at many business schools throughout the world, in spite of the fact that they are the most prevalent form of business organization and account for nearly 70 percent of employment in the United States and globally. This appears to be changing as more schools have recently added studies of entrepreneurship and family business to their curricula.

To appreciate the complex and emotionally vexing process of ever considering selling these companies or monetizing family wealth, it is helpful to understand the factors that have shaped their unique cultures and legacies.

Several frameworks and models designed to illuminate understanding of family companies have been developed by leading academics. The most widely accepted Three-Circle Model, which describes the family business system, was developed by Professor John A. Davis, chair of the Families in Business program at Harvard Business School, and his colleague, Professor Renato Tagiuri, in 1982.

Investor-owned companies have two major elements in their business structure: Owners and Employees. Some owners may work in the business, and some employees may be owners. (This structure is easy to understand and to manage.)

The family business system is far more complicated by adding the subsystem of family. We're all members of families, and we understand how family problems—between parents and children and between siblings and cousins—can occur and how emotions can flare. It can be wonderful, and it can be enormously difficult. When family is thrown into the mix—with issues, including money, employment, ownership, respect, fairness, and love—potential problems increase greatly.

Each of the circles in the following model represents a subsystem of the family business system.

Every individual who is part of a family business system can be placed in one of the seven spaces depicted by the three overlapping circles. Following are descriptions of those positions:

1. A member of the **Family** who does not own stock or work for the company
2. An **Owner** of stock in the company who is not a member of the family and does not work for the company

3. An employee of the **Business** who is not a member of the family and does not own stock
4. A **Family** member who is also an **Owner** of stock in the business
5. An employee of the **Business** who is also an **Owner** but not a family member
6. A **Family** member who works in the **Business** but does not own stock
7. A **Family** member who works in the **Business** and is an **Owner** of stock

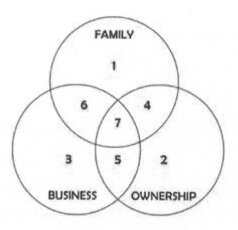

Tagiuri and Davis, 1982

The juxtaposition of individuals in the three-circle model sheds light on how conflict may be inherent in the system. An owner of the business who is not an employee will typically be more inclined to want to maximize financial returns, dividends, and return on investment. Employees, on the other hand, may be more interested in limiting dividends and maximizing reinvestment in the business to enhance personal income and career opportunities through growth and profitability. There may be issues among family members about who gets to work in the company and who doesn't. Compensation issues among employees can be a hot issue—but add family emotions, and it becomes hotter.

A family business system without an understanding of who fits where can only breed confusion. With no boundaries governing family, ownership rights, and management responsibilities, it would be chaos.

According to the landmark book *Generation to Generation,* each of the three subsystems—Business, Family, and Ownership—changes over time.

- Businesses progress through stages beginning with the start-up and struggle to survive and become profitable. This is followed by periods of stabilization and formalization of the business to accommodate the expansion that comes with profitability. Ultimately, the business matures and can be run as a cash cow as long as it lasts. Longevity requires infusion of new energy and reinvention of the business in response to changing times and conditions.

- Families grow up and generally move in different directions. In family business systems, they tend to stay together, bound by joint ownership of a valuable asset. Care must be given as the family grows and develops to create interest and attachment to the family company. Some members of the family become more involved through working in the company, acquiring ownership, and participating in governance structures.

- Ownership changes over time. The natural evolution of multigeneration, family-owned companies is from the Controlling Owner Stage to the Sibling Partnership Stage, where the founders or controlling owners pass ownership to their children. When the sibling generation passes their ownership to the next generation, the family business is in the cousin consortium stage. These ownership constellations can reverse course over time, such as when one family member purchases the shares of all the other family members and the company returns to a controlling owner stage.

The following Three-Dimensional Developmental Model illustrates the typical stages through which each of this family business systems pass.

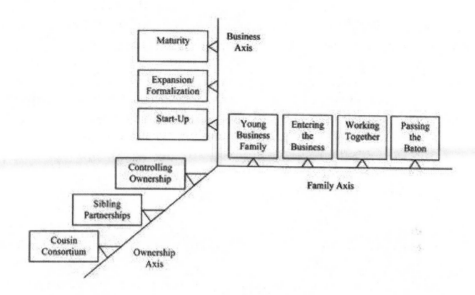

Each of these dimensions has an impact on the selling process. For example, as the Ownership System moves from the Controlling Owner to the Cousin Consortium stage, achieving agreement among various family members becomes more complex at each stage. There are simply more people involved in making critical decisions affecting the well-being of the family as well as resolving their own personal interests.

Looking at the Family System, companies have been most likely to sell at the Passing the Baton stage. When the leader of a family or the leader of the business is ready to step down, buyers may see a compelling void that might lead to a sale. In the Business System, companies in the start-up phase can be more difficult to sell than mature businesses with track records and predictable cash flows. Mature companies have a record of cash flows that can be indicative of the future. However, it's important to remember that while cash flow can be an important component of establishing a fair price, value is in the eye of the beholder—and therefore, a higher price will likely result if the seller is able to identify what's truly important to the buyer.

This Three-Dimensional Development Model provides a template that can be applied to any family business. In fact, it is a useful tool to begin the analysis of a family company as a first step in exploring the range of possibilities for monetizing and diversifying family wealth. While I am not an advocate of necessarily selling any company—like investment bankers, dealmakers, and financial advisors are—I feel that owners should be zealously focused on being informed and responsible stewards of family wealth. Transactions involving investor-owned companies are typically based solely on issues related to the business and risk/reward analysis among the investor/shareholders, the present situation, and future outlook. It's a whole different ball game in family companies. For some intermediaries and buyers, fully understanding family emotions about selling is confusing at best or an unsolvable equation or an irrational obstacle.

Prudent stewardship of ownership interests in family companies should include continuous monitoring of the competitive landscape and the strengths, weaknesses, opportunities, and threats companies face, along with a continuous search for the scalable golden nuggets in the company. This vigilance can ameliorate being blindsided by completely unforeseen events that can damage and even destroy the value of companies. The owners should be cognizant of the value of the enterprise in terms of return on equity and return on assets employed.

The circuitous route my dad took from young farmer to publishing entrepreneur and founder of two different and successful publishing companies—each successfully grown and carried on by one of his sons—is typical of the inventive founders of family companies like those honored recipients of the IMD—Lombard Odier Global Family Business Award.

As every family business succeeds and grows along each of the dimensions of business, family, and ownership, it is a useful exercise to periodically review its underlying legacy. Family companies are very different from investor-owned companies because of their stories—the ways in which the family's passion and commitment have shaped the development, culture, and success of the business.

The most successful companies I've studied are perpetually in the exploration phase of possibly selling and thereby maintain an acute awareness of the world in which they operate. Being in this phase is *not* paramount to having made or being compelled to make the decision to sell. It's simply a good business practice.

Following is a description of my own family's case using the Three-Dimensional Development Model as the template for analysis. This approach can easily be applied to any family company.

The Business System

Stage 1—Start-Up

George Pellegrin was the founder of several companies that ultimately led to the creation of Johnson Hill Press, our family's publishing company. As a young boy growing up in the suburbs of Chicago, my dad dreamed of creating a large-scale egg operation. Raising pigeons in his backyard fueled his passion for becoming a poultry farmer.

He saw opportunities easily. Early in his career, he developed innovative techniques for multiplying the yield of limited allocations of new seed varieties. He experimented with bypassing the conventional supply chains to achieve greater margins on the sale of commodity products.

My dad's father was his role model. Pa (the nickname my then three-year-old brother gave our paternal grandfather) had been an extraordinarily talented college athlete, a semi-pro football player, a successful independent industrial designer, and a good father. Dad saw him as a model of independence.

Pa gave Dad his start. He bought the first farm my dad operated from which his subsequent business activities germinated. His knack for bootstrapping ideas and borrowing money from banks allowed my dad to be a controlling owner of his venture and control his own destiny. As a serial entrepreneur, he ultimately created an ingenious publishing concept for the agricultural finance sector.

When my dad was farming, agriculture was becoming more and more capital intensive—requiring farmers to take on ever-increasing burdens of debt to keep up to date and survive. He was frustrated that the leading farm magazines were focused on production techniques—with little attention to either marketing or finance. He was struck that whenever he acquired a piece of farm machinery, it came with a thick manual devoted to its operation and maintenance. Seed was accompanied by specific planting instructions. Fertilizer came with directions about how to apply it safely and for maximum results. But there were no such instructions accompanying the ever-increasing amount of money—cash—he was borrowing. In this area he felt weakness. It took time for his latest business idea to come to fruition.

My dad's business interests and enterprises—ultimately leading to publishing—went through an evolution, like virtually all entrepreneurial and family businesses. What started as a small dairy farm grew into a diversified livestock operation. That transitioned into a beef cattle operation combined with becoming a large grower of small grain certified seed. The latter business grew into the nation's largest contract grower of small grain certified seed at the time. This business evolved into an ill-fated attempt to compete with Quaker Oats Company in the manufacture of oatmeal for consumers. In order to avert bankruptcy, his survival skills led him into the grain elevator business in order to utilize his plant facilities and the manufacture of *Holi Boli* games to use up thousands of small tin cans he had purchased for exporting his oatmeal to international markets. He sold the entire inventory—thousands of *Holi Boli* games, each containing ten tin cans originally intended to be vacuum-sealed containers of rolled oats—to a single retail store led by a fellow entrepreneur. The customer, Allens' Merchandising, was perhaps the original Sam's Club, complete with a requirement that customers have a membership card to enter the store and be able to buy in larger quantities at discounted prices.

To liquidate the inventory of oatmeal that was being returned from the supermarkets because it wasn't selling, my brother and I spent months after school and on weekends breaking open cases of small ($0.10 retail value) tubes of oatmeal and then opening and dumping the contents of the tiny tubes into a large hopper that carried the oatmeal down a conveyor belt into fifty-pound burlap bags. Dad had presold the fifty-pound bags of oatmeal to a feedlot operation for consumption by cattle. It is an excellent example of *reverse* value added!

Launching the Family Publishing Business

After tying up the loose ends of his failed companies—Pell Bari Farms and Pilgrim Mills—Dad began to look for a new venture. He was somehow reminded of the unmet need he had earlier identified for financial management information tailored to farmers. He visualized a regular frequency publication containing a curriculum of practical and useful content focused on the prudent and profitable use of borrowed money in farm operations.

He launched his magazine in 1957. Today, the formula he developed seems simple, but fifty years ago, before the application of computer technology to prepress, printing, binding, and mailing operations, it wasn't easy. Early on, when Dad took his idea to publishers and printers, he was told it was far too complicated, had too many moving parts, and would be impossible to execute.

Certainly, there were cumbersome logistical issues associated with his project, but its underlying concept was elegantly simple and logical. He was not dissuaded from figuring out a way to produce the magazine, assuming he could generate adequate revenue.

In the 1930s, the federal government provided seed money to create a cooperative credit organization to exclusively serve the agricultural market. As capital needs for farmers were growing, both public and private sector leaders recognized the need to develop a reliable lending source for farmers—to insure the availability of an abundant food supply and to guarantee the United States' position as a leading exporter of food commodities in the world market. One of the three branches of the Farm Credit System included a network of some four hundred local Production Credit Associations chartered to provide short and intermediate term loans to farmers. An affiliated group of Federal Intermediate Credit Banks was responsible for raising the money needed to fund the PCA loans through the sale of debentures in the major money markets. In effect, the twelve Federal Intermediate Credit Banks (FICBs) were the discount banks for the PCAs in their respective districts. The country was divided into twelve districts mirroring those of the Federal Reserve Banks.

Each of the four hundred PCAs had a fair amount of autonomy as independent local cooperatives owned by their farmers/borrowers/members. They were governed by a local board of directors and within broad guidelines operated autonomously. Therefore, there were philosophical and operating differences—some substantial—among the individual PCAs. Each PCA was governed by a board of directors composed of farmers/borrowers in the local area, and the PCAs in each district collectively owned their Federal Intermediate Credit Bank. It was a difficult system to navigate in order to create a sustainable revenue stream for a fledgling magazine, but my dad persevered and was ultimately successful.

PCAs extended credit to farmers in their designated territories. Farmers used the money for equipment purchases, supplies, and working capital—to provide liquidity during the cycles between planting, harvesting, and marketing their commodities. Therefore, the bulk of the borrowed cash was circulated by the farmers to agribusinesses in the local markets served by the PCAs. The 1950s through the early 1980s were extraordinary growth years for American agriculture, and during this boom period, PCAs became the dominant provider of short and intermediate term credit to farmers, eclipsing the position long held by local country banks.

Dad's first operating loan in 1938 came from the local PCA in Woodstock, Illinois. Through his experience as a borrower/member, he learned about the Farm Credit System and challenges it faced communicating for the system as a whole. He saw that it had been impossible to deliver a uniform message that accurately addressed varied needs of the individual entities comprising the aggregate system. This conundrum provided the perfect opportunity to develop an innovative publishing model.

He created a magazine with national editorial content focused on the responsible and profitable use of borrowed money. It also included regional editorial sections that addressed the regional idiosyncrasies of US agriculture, local sections for news from each individual PCA, and local advertising pages for retailers of farm machinery, feed, fertilizer, and supplies only purchased by farmers. My dad pioneered this innovative publishing concept.

The Business System
Stage 2—Expansion/Formalization
Dad's business was serving critical educational and communications needs for the growing Farm Credit System, and his enterprise was taking on a life of its own. It was growing rapidly as more PCAs purchased

subscriptions of the magazine for their borrowers and prospective borrowers. He expanded his product line to include more marketing communications and printing services the PCAs required.

In fact, the business was becoming a valuable asset in and of itself as it continued to grow beyond my dad's craft of being a creative, persuasive salesman with solid understanding and expertise in his served market. Each new customer fueled revenue growth and provided exceptional marginal contribution to the overhead and profit of the business. His idea became well established, growing in revenue, profit, and number of employees. It had become profitable, sustainable, and scalable—three key factors to building a valuable and saleable company.

My dad loved the business and everything about it—his customers, his employees, and developing all the processes that made it work efficiently and profitably. He brought ingenuity to every aspect of the business, and he was unabashedly passionate about his creation. In his mind the company would never be sold. It was like a child to which he had incredible attachment.

Eleven years after it was founded, I joined the company to assist my dad with his sales and marketing responsibilities. It didn't take long before I discovered the real golden nugget that would fuel our company's growth.

I recognized that the uniqueness of *PCA Farming* could be replicated in other markets. The idea was to identify precisely defined target markets with specialized information needs to aid in the purchase decisions of high-value products that were supplied by independent distributors and local retail dealers. Creating publications with tightly focused editorial content, published in regional editions to reflect geographic and demographic differences, and localized for the independent retail dealers provided the basis for a very unique marketing communications vehicle for suppliers in our targeted markets. Indeed, it turned out to be a winning combination.

By this time, we had perfected the processes—identifying markets and gathering circulation lists; preparing highly focused editorial content; producing and printing high-quality publications; selling national, regional, and local advertising products; and creating systems to invoice and collect money from thousands of relatively small customers.

The Business System

Stage 3—Maturity

Successor-owners of our family company are still following the fundamental processes created by my dad more than fifty years ago and further developed and refined in the ensuing years by our team and me.

While Johnson Hill Press was well organized with a talented staff and financial performance beginning to look like a healthy and secure annuity, the plethora of open markets and gaps for our company to exploit with new magazines began to diminish in the late '80s and early '90s. Other companies in our industry had begun emulating our unique approach to publishing. This increased competition was creating pressure on pricing, and our ability to create truly unique publishing products was becoming more challenging. It seemed like the trade magazine business was becoming commoditized. Our company, while midsized in our industry, was among the most profitable; however, the nascent Internet and its potential impact on print publishing were becoming a very real threat.

The game had changed for us from organic growth, gaining market share, and starting innovative new magazines to participating in the industry consolidation and continuing growth through acquisitions to lower costs of production. By the mid-1990s our industry was dominated by companies with much deeper pockets using "other people's money" and with higher investment risk profiles than we had. This mix of factors, *combined with my losing passion for the business,* contributed to our decision to sell the family company in 1994. Our company was in need of another wealth creator with unbounded passion and enthusiasm for the business in order to begin growing again, to say nothing of the need for fresh energy.

It's worth noting that the maturity stage of a business is a particularly dangerous stage. While cash flow can be maximized, decline ultimately is an inevitable part of the business life cycle. Increasing cash flow as investment requirements diminish masks future problems as the company begins to suffer from the lack of innovation. That said, it could be a good time to sell to an acquirer that is consolidating the industry. It's a time when both profits and cash flow are excellent.

The Family System

Stage 1—Young Business Family

While I didn't share my dad's interest in sports and wasn't gifted with natural athletic ability, I did share his interest in business. Perhaps it was my pathway for a closer connection to him, as baseball was for my brother. But that's another topic, best left for psychoanalysis.

From childhood, I admired my dad's business skills. I loved going to the office with him on Saturday mornings and even wore a miniature copy of his company's khaki uniform to school when I was six years old and in first grade. My name was embroidered over the shirt pocket just like all the people who worked at the company. Some of the kids made fun of me, but I didn't care. I was proud to be a part of Pell Bari Farms.

I spent several summers working in the various businesses my dad had. I loved the environment and enjoyed the work. Early on, I understood the basic economic equation—sell things for more than *all* of the costs. I think he liked the interest I exhibited and was generally happy to have me around.

Beginning in elementary school and continuing through college, I started several little businesses myself—a few of which employed friends. My entrepreneurial interests paralleled my dad's and seemed to draw us together, despite frequently feeling like I disappointed him because of my lack of interest in sports and my weak academic performance compared with my older brother.

I was fourteen when my dad started *PCA Farming* and founded his publishing company. My brother and I were keenly aware of the failure of the oatmeal business. When I was eleven years old, I have recollections of hanging out in the breakfast cereal section of the local Piggly Wiggly supermarket waiting, watching, and hoping shoppers would put the small, attractive packages of Pilgrim Oats in their shopping carts. (The English word "pilgrim" translated to French is *pelerin*. My dad's ancestors were from the French-speaking part of Belgium.) I was always sad when I left the supermarket because my empirical studies certainly didn't portend success.

My disappointment about the ill-fated oatmeal business turned to enthusiasm and pride in *PCA Farming* and what my dad was accomplishing. Having spent my early years doing chores on our family farm, I understood the rudiments of the magazine.

There was a huge map mounted on the wall of Dad's office. Pins on the map identified each of four hundred PCAs that served more than three thousand counties in the country. Dad's customers, the PCAs that were sending subscriptions of his magazine to their borrowers/members, were identified with green pins; and as Dad used to say, the ones who hadn't yet "seen the light" were identified with red pins. It was a Saturday morning ritual for me to accompany him to the office and see him triumphantly pull out several red pins and replace them with green ones. He always had a big smile when he was doing this, and I shared his pride for the week's accomplishment. I also knew that converting red pins to green ones boded well for our family's finances and my dad's general disposition.

In high school when I received an award for selling the most advertising in our school's athletic programs, there seemed to be a real converging of Dad's and my interests and skill sets.

I worked my way through college in a number of interesting jobs, enjoying them more than my classes, with the exception of those subjects that related to my work. When I received the award for being the outstanding advertising student in my junior year of college, the professor who presented me with the award quickly pointed out that it wasn't because of my grades, but rather because of my ability to apply what I had learned in the classroom to the campus merchants who were my customers.

The Family System
Stage 2—Entering the Family Business

After spending two years doing market research and business development for a Midwest-based chain of radio and television stations and a year in New York with a leading department store operation, my dad invited me to join his small publishing company and move back to a rural town in Wisconsin. He had been impressed with the work experience I was accumulating, and he felt his company could benefit from my drive and capabilities.

At first I was reluctant, and I think that disappointed him. My career was going well in New York—three rapid promotions in my first year and growing visibility with the top executives. While my dad's offer was flattering, I didn't feel ready to make a move. I think I felt like being in New York, half a continent away from Wisconsin, and succeeding in one of the toughest, most competitive markets in the world were really establishing my credentials. I was gaining tremendous confidence at a very young age, independent of my family.

Seeing my reticence, Chet Bell, my dad's financial partner (who was not active in the management of the publishing business), came to New York to sell me on the idea of accepting the offer. He expressed his optimism and vision for the company and persuaded me that I could play an integral part of an amazing success story. It was a good strategy—an independent person who I respected was advising me on the merits of the opportunity and how much I was really needed.

My brother was in the military at the time, stationed at Fort Dix in New Jersey. He came down to New York one weekend while I was struggling with the choices facing me. He asked me, "If you stay where you are, what position do you aspire to?"

I replied, "Executive vice president—general merchandising manager."

He asked, "How long do you think it will take to get there? What are your chances for being selected? Why aren't you aspiring to become president of the company?"

I responded, "Most likely about twenty-five years to become EVP—GMM, and I think I would have fifty-fifty chance of making it." (I was pretty cocky!) "I would be an unlikely candidate for president because that position had always been filled by a member of the ownership family."

Then he said, "To what job would you aspire at Dad's company, and what are your chances for achieving it?"

I understood, and I had a new perspective with which to evaluate my alternatives. There was a real job available back in Wisconsin. If I didn't accept it, someone else would, so it was time for longer-term thinking. In that context, I was happy with the opportunity that was being offered to me, and I accepted. My starting date was two months off.

The Family System

Stage 3—Working Together

All of my previous experiences prepared me for my new job as director of marketing services at Johnson Hill Press in Fort Atkinson, Wisconsin. Selling skills I had learned in retail stores, selling ads in athletic programs, working for the newspaper, the radio and television stations, and publishing my own magazine, *Wisconsin Man*, while a student at the University of Wisconsin, provided the perfect background for exceeding expectations of my new employer. The market research and sales promotion experiences I had at the *Milwaukee Journal/Sentinel* and Midcontinent Broadcasting Company were directly applicable, and my experience in the retail business gave me an uncommon understanding of our customers and prospective customers. I hit the ground running.

My dad and I had a wonderful six-year run. We worked together well, and I felt I was learning a lot and growing. It was an exciting time—working together on the development of creative ideas and seeing the business grow. I had a knack for starting new magazines that quickly turned a profit. Our relationship was underscored by not only love but also complete trust in one another. The seventh and eighth years, however, became increasingly problematic—I viewed Johnson Hill Press differently than my dad did. Father-son disagreements about the direction of the company were festering and finally led to my decision to leave. My dad hadn't changed; I had. He was still a great boss, leaving me alone to do my job and providing plenty of encouragement and praise along the way. He was seldom critical of my performance.

It was me. I was critical of him and the bad decisions I felt he was making. I was second-guessing nearly everything he was doing. His nose wasn't in my job; my nose was in his. Now, I can see, it must have been impossible for him! I saw a scalable business—one that could grow substantially but no longer as an extension of the founder's vision. Dad preferred to run it the way he wanted to run it, in spite of the fact that it was inhibiting the growth potential I saw and cutting into profitability. That was certainly his prerogative, but I couldn't stand it. He tended to become infatuated with all kinds of ideas and possibilities without regard to required capital investments and the real returns they would generate in the short and long term. Always optimistic, he consistently overestimated sales and underestimated costs—a horrible combination. He was infinitely creative, and in my judgment that attribute got in the way of making good business decisions. His superb selling skills and personal charm, combined with his inventive qualities, were assets as well as liabilities in his career. Naturally, he didn't see it that way.

My frustration with the status quo had reached a level that was no longer tolerable for me, so I had to go.

The Family System

Stage 4—Passing the Baton

The Harvard Business School Case begins:

Jon Pellegrin walked solemnly into his father's office on Friday afternoon, October 1, 1976. He had spent many weeks thinking about this conversation. He didn't want this to happen but also couldn't postpone it any longer. Jon slumped into the chair opposite George's desk and started talking when his father looked up from the mounds of paper on his desk. "Dad, we both know this isn't working and it's getting worse. I can't handle it any longer; I really don't think you can either." George shifted in his chair as he looked at his son. He was used to having frank talks with Jonathan. George knew he needed to listen. Jon continued, "This is your company. You started it, and there's no reason you should leave. You love the business and you're obviously too young to retire. But our differences about how to run the company are getting bigger, and our relationship is deteriorating quickly.

"DeeDee and I have spent the last four months seriously considering our options, and we've finally decided that we're ready to leave. I'm going to apply for the White House Fellows program and I've been told I will be accepted. We'll go to Washington for a year or two, and after that time I'm sure there will be other opportunities." George nodded thoughtfully at what Jon was saying, but said nothing.

"Dad, I know that you are going to have to make some changes in staffing, and I understand that I may be foreclosing the chance to ever come back. I'm ready to make that choice now. I am willing to sell you

back the stock in the company which you sold me three years ago at exactly what I paid for it." Jon was now silent, waiting for a response."

The case study concludes with George Pellegrin's decision to pass the baton of leadership to Jonathan and step away from an active management role at *his* company. His decision and subsequent actions marked the transition of Johnson Hill Press from a founder-managed entrepreneurial venture to the beginning of a true multigeneration family business. George's previous thirty-eight years had been spent first as a craftsman—a farmer—and subsequently as a serial entrepreneur, starting a number of small businesses and reinventing others to respond to market needs he identified.

———

At that point of time in my life, I was brimming with self-confidence and even arrogance. I had been working in the company for eight years, launched more than a half dozen profitable magazines, served on the board of directors of the National Agri-Marketing Association, was president of the Wisconsin Chapter, led two very successful trade missions to Africa on behalf of the US Department of Commerce, and had been invited to apply for the White House Fellows program by Rogers Morton, the then secretary of commerce.

During a recent class discussion of our case at Harvard Business School, one earnest young student opined, "This is awful; Jonathan's father not only gave him a job, but he gave him life itself. How could he threaten to leave and do this to his father?"

It was a good point. After all, I was thirty-two years old at the time.

This story could have unfolded in any number of ways. George could have encouraged me to go to Washington and revisited questions of succession after my work experience in government. Perhaps establishing a more precise succession plan would have influenced my level of patience. Or the company could have been divided into separate divisions, subsidiaries, or even separate companies with different shareholder compositions—thereby making a split in responsibilities between the two of us clearer. He could have written me off as to any future interest and hired my replacement and his heir apparent. He could have begun exploring the possibility of an Employee Stock Ownership Plan as another alternative to passing on his ownership interest at some future point and monetizing his life's work. He also could have made the decision to sell the company. These kinds of questions face all family companies as they approach critical crossroads.

It was the biggest surprise of my life when he and my mother invited my wife and me to their home on Sunday afternoon (following my Friday afternoon resignation) to ask us if my decision about leaving the company would be different if Dad chose to leave. I didn't know how to react. Of course, I would feel different, but I absolutely did not want to force him out of his company. Going to Washington was an exceptional alternative, and I was ready to go. However, the opportunity to succeed my father as the leader of our company and pursue *my* vision for the business was more appealing than spending time in government. Dad's confidence in my ability, experience, and track record in the business, along with strong encouragement from my mother, Dorothy, and his financial partner, Chet Bell, helped him work through the vexing decision to turn over to me the CEO position of the company he had founded and loved. It was, indeed, both a courageous and generous step—uncommon among most entrepreneurs, business founders, and controlling owners.

It wasn't until my father and I had worked together full time for six years that I began to see his limitations. Based on our respective ages and life stages, our father-son collision was predictable as John Davis proved in his landmark Harvard Business School doctoral dissertation—*Life Stages and Their Effect on Father-Son Work Relationships.*

Today, there are excellent courses that instruct families how to develop and execute succession plans, like the Families in Business program at Harvard Business School. There were no such courses available to my father and me to provide insight into the best practices of well-run family companies. The success in our family company's generational transition must be credited to my father for his extraordinary intuition and his willingness to step aside at a time when he was really not ready to do so.

After Dad's big announcement about appointing me president and his decision to step back, nothing changed. For several days he continued coming to work at the same time, doing the same things, meeting with the same people, and leaving at the same time at day's end.

To me, my promotion looked like a sham! Fortunately, I had not yet closed the door on the White House Fellow opportunity.

My Dad explained that in his view the company had problems that he wanted to fix before his departure. I explained that I knew about the problems, and I had to fix them, if I was, in fact, the leader of the company. I told him there was still time for him to reconsider his decision, and I would be happy to leave.

Within two hours he had packed up his personal things and left his office for the last time. Watching him leave the company he had founded was bittersweet and deeply touching.

Then fate intervened. My brother called my dad and told him that the parent company, which owned *Honolulu* magazine, had just gone into bankruptcy and would be selling off assets—of which the magazine was likely to be one of the first to go.

Dad called his financial partner, Chet Bell, and they were off on the next plane to Hawaii.

My brother had gone to graduate school at the East-West Center at the University of Hawaii and stayed, becoming a journalist for the leading local newspaper after a stint with Associated Press in China. His career dream was to own and publish *Honolulu* magazine. At the time he called Dad about *Honolulu* magazine, he was completing a one-year assignment as a UNESCO advisor to the Caribbean News Agency—the wire service serving newspapers and broadcast outlets with news from the Caribbean islands.

In just four months, Honolulu Publishing Company was established as a subsidiary of Johnson Hill Press for the purpose of acquiring *Honolulu* magazine. My parents packed up their belongings in Wisconsin and moved to Honolulu where he became CEO of the subsidiary company.

For sure, the management transition between my father and me was eased by his involvement in a brand-new enterprise more than four thousand miles away.

In the ensuing two years, the sales volume of Johnson Hill Press more than doubled, and profit quadrupled while employment was reduced by nearly 20 percent. The company was on a roll.

The Ownership System

> *The ownership of every family company will change over time—whether through generational transfer or outright sale. Therefore, <u>every business is going to be sold</u>—it's ultimately just a matter of when, how, to whom, and the terms and conditions. The implied imperative is that the owners of family companies must be responsible shareholders and continually monitor the value of their companies through that lens. This means the business is more than "what the family does" ... it is an asset requiring responsible and informed stewardship.*
> *—JONATHAN PELLEGRIN, 1996*

Stage 1—Controlling Owner

After losing all his money and all of my grandfather's money in his ill-fated oatmeal business, like many entrepreneurs and company founders, "necessity became the mother of invention" for my dad. Having been independent all his life, he just couldn't fathom working for someone else. So, he bootstrapped the development of his publishing business. While he had investors along the way, he was always the controlling owner.

Chet Bell, my dad's financial partner for many years, was the perfect complement to my dad. My dad was clearly in charge; however, Chet provided a much-needed balance and was able to provide the guidance and offer suggestions that my dad always felt were his own. They had amazing respect for one other. Chet never worked in the business; however, they both loved the time they spent together as confidants and mutual sounding boards, and until the day Chet died, they never had a single disagreement.

In 1973 when my dad sold me half of his stock in the company, he was still the controlling owner as most family business patriarchs are, even though they are generous with the distribution of their stock to family members. And when I was ready to leave the company, I was prepared to return my stock to my dad for exactly what I had paid for it, in spite of its increased value.

The *controlling owner* stage of a business is the easiest to navigate. The owner makes the decisions — no arguments! It's the "Golden Rule" in full play — "He who has the gold rules."

The biggest impediments to generational continuity beyond the controlling owner stage are as follows:

1. There is no talented leader who can step into the shoes of the controlling owner and lead the company through the next generation.
2. The founder/family patriarch may not be best role model or mentor for the succeeding CEO of a sibling partnership. CEO successors must become "servant leaders" in order to succeed.
3. The controlling owner is unable to "let go" so his or her successor can assume the leadership of the company without the invasiveness of the previous leader.
4. The sibling partners are unable to accept and support the new leader(s).

When we entered into an agreement to purchase Chet Bell's ownership interest ten years after I joined the company, a market value for the company was established. The company paid some of the proceeds in cash at closing, plus a seven-year note to Chet paid the remainder.

When ownership of a family company is transferred, I firmly believe the selling shareholder should be paid out and therefore have no ongoing ownership of the company. The purchasers should have full responsibility for the success and failure of the company and for any and all debt incurred in the process of buying stock.

Price, terms, and conditions of any *internal* sale must be structured so the buyer is able to service the debt.

In our family's case, my dad eliminated any potential problems in the sibling partnership stage by making it possible for both my brother and me to become controlling owners by splitting the company in two—my brother's in Hawaii and mine based in Wisconsin.

The Ownership System
Stage 2—Sibling Partnership
This is the most problematic stage of the ownership system. Parents love their children equally, and their decisions are virtually always based on

what they perceive as fairness—financial equality for each child. Believe it or not, many parents believe their companies can be successfully operated by the next generation of siblings working as a committee of equals. This rarely works. There needs to be a boss, one who can make decisions and avoid gridlock.

But how can one sibling be selected over another? It's just not fair. The controlling owner built his company for the benefit of all his children—equally. So how can he pick one to lead his company over the others?

One way to approach this issue is to make ownership available only to those who work in the company. But if more than one child wants to work in the company, the problem of selecting the leader persists.

Following is a suggestion that has worked effectively in selecting the CEO of a sibling partnership.

Two to three years before the controlling owner is truly ready to step down, there are some actions that can be helpful in the transition. It is imperative that the controlling owner *be ready* to step aside in two years' time from his or her announcement about leaving active management of the company.

1. A high-functioning board of directors with nonfamily members should be put in place. No family member other than the controlling owner should be on the board so that frank and honest discussions can take place about succession. Members might include another controlling owner of a comparable size company. Another member should be a successful CEO of a sibling partnership company. The third outside board member should have experience in the industry in which the company operates.
2. All of the siblings with even the remote potential to lead the company should attend the Leadership Development Program at the Center for Creative Leadership headquartered in Greensboro, North Carolina.
3. A year after the CEO candidates have completed the leadership course, the leading candidate should be enrolled in the Leading for Organizational Impact program (also offered by CCL) designed to help CEOs get ready to assume the top leadership

position. It shouldn't take more than a year, or two at the most, for the board of directors to make an informed choice as to whether or not the chosen candidate is "ready enough" to assume the mantle of leadership. The retiring leader should then sever his or her relationship with the company. The successor can always call the retired leader if he or she needs advice or counsel. It's much better if advice is solicited rather than imposed.

The Ownership System

Stage 3—Cousin Consortium

Managing the diversity of such an ownership group can be very complex. At this stage, *structure* is the best friend of the family. It can come on three levels—the family assembly (including all family members), the family council (only family members elected by the family assembly), and the board of directors (elected by the shareholders of the company, with a blend of both family owners and talented, experienced outsiders).

Much has been written about family governance, but suffice it to say, the family assembly helps to keep camaraderie and unity in the family. The family council plans and executes activities and events for the family assembly and interfaces with the board of directors to keep family members apprised of news at the company. The board of directors is responsible for protecting the interests of the shareholders and maintaining a high-level view of the company, including strategy and hiring and firing of the chief executive officer.

When a company reaches the cousin consortium stage, many options for ownership emerge. Because of the age and long-term performance of the enterprise, the book value of the company is generally large. This affords the opportunity for the firm to establish an internal stock market and facilitate the purchase of stock from disinterested owners. Sale and transfer of shares may be arranged for family owners interested in selling. There are other alternatives depending on the financial strength of the company. The stock of selling shareholders can be purchased by the company and held as *treasury stock*.

Consistent communication with all shareholders and stakeholders is imperative in the Cousin Consortium stage. Big decisions like selling the business will require approvals. If the company is in play and receives offers, a market value is established.

Once this happens, it is possible for shareholders who want to sell to be able to do so, while at the same time, shareholders who don't want to sell don't have to. But it's important to know that internal stock purchase plans can result in incurring debt. That results in risk and the reduction of investment capital in the company.

The specter of owning a company with substantial "stock purchase" debt may cause more shareholders to want to monetize their shareholdings through a sale. The offering price from an outsider may be too large, prohibiting the possibility of choice, which is exactly what happened to the Bancroft family when Rupert Murdoch offered to buy the *Wall Street Journal* for more than five billion dollars. History has proven the wisdom of the Bancroft family's decision to sell.

Family Wealth

In recent years, the study of family business has expanded from operational, succession, and governance issues to overall stewardship of family wealth. Inherent in this exploration is the unambiguous fact that the *family company* is typically the largest single asset a *business family* owns. It can represent 90 percent of a family's total wealth, and if it is privately owned, it can be an illiquid asset. As time goes on, owners need to also expand their thinking from one of being operators of a company to being stewards of family wealth. This opens Pandora's box, and the family company may no longer be considered an asset that will *never* be sold. The family business is an asset in a portfolio and should be evaluated in an informed manner for the benefit of the shareholders (and future shareholders).

There's a very long-term nature to the way families think and work. John Davis, a leader in the study of family business, has led the field in thinking about what drives success and *sustainability*. Growth and unity are fundamental to both the success of families and their businesses, but now the focus has to be on everything encompassing the family enterprise—all holdings—and the sustainability of each and every asset in every family's portfolio in order to achieve continuity for the business family.

Momentum is a big factor in the ongoing success of any organization; it's the sense of positive forward movement. Once that's lost in any group, bad things start to happen. People become anxious and threatened. They become worried about their future and don't trust that being together is moving them ahead any longer.

Just as the founders and succeeding generations' builders of companies created wealth, families need a "wealth creator" in *every generation*. Families tend to grow faster than businesses, so new wealth has to be created in addition to returns on traditional investment alternatives. There are many stories of families unconsciously or unknowingly liquidating their companies by spending more than their assets generate. Financial transparency and education are essential in developing healthy business families that can be sustained.

Successful stewards of wealth are attuned to evaluating the strengths, weaknesses, opportunities, and threats of all their businesses and other financial investments. Continual evaluation is prudent. At any given time, responsible stewards should ask the following questions: Should this asset be held or sold? If it's sold, what asset(s) should be bought to replace it?

What Is the Definition of a Successful Sale?

A big factor in making the decision to sell is most often driven by underlying fear. It can be rooted in the possibility of something untoward happening that might impair the financial health of the company. Wealthy individuals and families, whose assets are concentrated rather than having a more diversified portfolio, may be taking on more risk than is prudent over the long term.

> *Diversification aims to maximize return by investing in different areas that would each react differently to the same event. Most investment professionals agree that, although it does not guarantee against loss, diversification is the most important component of reaching long-range financial goals while minimizing risk.*
> —INVESTOPEDIA, *JULY 1, 2016*

Time and again it has been demonstrated that diversification can be dangerous *for companies* that pursue opportunities that may not be suited to their experience and core competencies. But research has proven that diversification *for individual investors* has reduced risk and enhanced returns over the long term.

At the end of day, buyers can do whatever they want to do with companies they purchase in spite of their representations and promises to sellers. *Therefore, in my judgment, a successful sale is one that achieves the maximum price, paid in cash at closing.*

There are many techniques that sellers can use to improve their chances for achieving a successful sale. There are even more possibilities of things that can go wrong that make it difficult to successfully complete the sale. Both will be covered in future chapters.

According to the 2016 Family Business Survey, conducted by Price Waterhouse Coopers, the vast majority of family business owners indicate that ownership of the company will change. (*In fact, the ownership of every family company will change over time.*) Most suggest that stock will be transferred to the next generation, and a diminishing percentage of succeeding generations indicates there are any plans to sell the company.

Logical questions include the following:

- What if the next generation has neither the capability nor the desire to own the family business?
- What if the fundamentals of the business are changing so it is no longer building wealth for the family but is actually destroying wealth?
- What if continued ownership does not seem to make economic sense over the long haul?

Given the fact that ownership will change in the future, current owners have to make appropriate decisions about all the assets in the family's estate and therefore make informed decisions about keeping or selling assets in the estate. Sweeping statements and forever commitments by owners regarding significant assets are no longer either relevant or responsible.

Following are the current plans according to the Price Waterhouse Coopers study:

In the first generation:

1. Thirty percent of the owners plan to pass ownership to the next generation.
2. Twenty-nine percent plan to pass on ownership but bring in professional management.
3. Twenty-nine percent plan to sell the company or bring in outside shareholders.

In the second generation:

1. Forty-one percent of the shareholders plan to pass ownership to the next generation.
2. Thirty-six percent plan to pass on ownership but bring in professional management.
3. Fourteen percent plan to sell the company or bring in outside shareholders.

In the third generation:

1. Forty-three percent of the shareholders plan to pass ownership to the next generation.
2. Thirty-eight percent plan to pass on ownership but bring in professional management.
3. Nine percent plan to sell the company or bring in outside shareholders.

In the fourth generation:

1. Forty-six percent of the shareholders plan to pass ownership to the next generation.
2. Thirty-six percent plan to pass on ownership but bring in professional management.
3. Six percent plan to sell the company or bring in outside shareholders.

In the fifth generation:

1. Fifty-two percent of the shareholders plan to pass ownership to the next generation.
2. Thirty-four percent plan to pass on ownership but bring in professional management.
3. Five percent plan to sell the company or bring in outside shareholders.

In every generational transition, ownership changes hands. There are many issues that need to be considered. Among them are valuation, monetizing the retiring generation, tax considerations, and many more.

CHAPTER 2

CHALLENGES OF SELLING YOUR FAMILY BUSINESS

Selling public companies and investor-owned companies is pretty straightforward devoid of emotions. The objective, first, last, and always, has been to maximize shareholder value. Selling is a matter of performance, outlook, and timing.

On the other hand, there are complexities in selling family companies that are, at best, difficult to understand. They are about balancing the needs and wants of individual owners and family members of multiple generations, and they are not all about shareholder value and money.

Sellers can lose sight of just how long and complicated the process of exploring and making the decision to sell can take. While it may seem purely intuitive, there are many steps in the entire process of selling whether the seller has awareness of them or not.

The exploration period can be very interesting and even fun. There are no commitments—only learning and benchmarking. Exploratory conversations with trusted mentors, friends who sold companies or bought companies, investment bankers, private equity firms, commercial bankers, accountants, and lawyers all can be illuminating. There is no obligation to do anything, and the only limitation on sellers is the depth of their curiosity.

On the other hand, the decision-making period is much tougher. Wrestling with issues concerning the wisdom of selling from a strictly business perspective requires careful economic, strategic, and operational analysis. Adding the emotional dimension of family considerations, particularly in cases where there may be differences of opinion about selling or not selling as well as varied feelings about the capabilities of various family members, creates more complexity. Personal feelings about continuing ownership of the business or selling out, which are rooted in the volatile psychological matrix of passion, fear, anxiety, loyalty, shame, doubt, confidence, and a myriad of other thoughts, can make reaching the decision to sell extraordinarily difficult.

Once reached, however, sellers typically sigh with relief that they've finally decided! They may have spent more emotional energy on this decision than any other in their lives.

At this point—when the decision to sell has been reached—it's pretty easy for the owners to begin thinking about what they might be moving toward rather than where they are now. Knowing that their previously illiquid asset is going to be monetized, it's hard not to think about how they might want to spend some of their money and how they might want to change their lifestyle. This can be dangerous.

Recent studies about families losing wealth due to the decline of their once successful family companies have led some families to consider selling their companies or divisions or subsidiaries of their companies or even product lines in order to monetize some of their assets and diversify their holdings to better protect their wealth over the long term.

While family companies have created enormous wealth for business families, protection of wealth over generations may be done more effectively through a diversified portfolio of assets. This is particularly true when there are no wealth creators involved in the family business. Wealth management is becoming the primary area of study for more and more academics and consultants to wealthy families.

This new frontier has made the decisions facing business families far more difficult than they were in the past. But still discussions about selling can be a taboo subject.

Issues of loyalty, legacy, pride, tradition, passion, and others make conversations among family members uncomfortable. Deteriorating financial performance, loss of market share and industry position, debilitating price wars, and new technology requiring massive capital investments can lead families to begin discussing the taboo subject. Other weaknesses can be uncovered, including lack of talent to lead the company forward and the need for new blood and energy in the business.

An active merger and acquisition market with high valuations add fuel to potential considerations of selling.

Individual family members may have very different goals, objectives, and views about owning the family company. Getting on the same page about selling doesn't necessarily mean agreeing. There are many possibilities, including reaching an agreement where family members who want to sell are able to do so, while family members who *don't* may have the opportunity to keep (and possibly increase) their ownership stake, but they will also increase their risk of ownership. Some cases were great successes for those who wanted to continue owning the company, while others were complete disasters where the value of the company completely vaporized after the transaction was completed. Typically, excessive debt incurred to take out the selling shareholders was a major cause of the failure.

The principal shareholders—family and business leaders—seem to have a huge struggle considering whether or not to sell. Reality is that at some point their stock will no longer belong to them. The extreme reason is death. Actively considering what happens to the ownership of the company is an important responsibility for controlling owners, sibling partners, and cousin-owners. It's a stewardship issue, and there are far more complications passing *a company* from generation to generation than passing *financial assets like cash* and fungible assets that can be readily divided and more easily traded. Passing a business to succeeding generations can, in some cases, be more of a burden than a benefit and may put a valuable asset at greater risk in the future.

Most family members have never gone through a major sale and therefore tend to oversimplify the process.

Oversimplification

Consequences of not thinking deeply about the decision to sell can be disastrous. It is critical to fully understand all the dimensions of making an informed decision to sell. Not doing it carefully can cause irreparable harm to the family as well as to the company. Interviews with business families around the world, who had either sold their companies or were contemplating doing so, had tremendous similarity. At first the explanations seemed rational and logical. Beginning with business issues, including industry dynamics and business life cycles, there were solid considerations that favored selling. There were discussions about competition and potential threats to the continued success of the business that colored the conversations. And they always ended with an analysis of the family, particularly succeeding generations and their levels of interest in carrying on the business and perceptions of their capabilities to do so.

In conversations, I had to reveal much about my own family and our experiences before I could break through the surface of the shallow but seemingly rational explanations for the decisions the families made. There was usually less rational thinking that tipped the scale in the decision making.

The work of Sigmund Freud, considered the father of psychoanalysis, and Carl Jung, the founder of analytical psychology, provide excellent templates for approaching the decision. Awareness of the deeper issues may help both sellers and buyers of these companies understand the complexity of making decisions to sell or not.

In every case I studied, the decisions were rooted in the family's *passion* for the business and a complex combination of *fear, fright, and anxiety*, to say nothing of *guilt* and possibly *shame*. *Passion* comprises the energy, drive, and joy that create, sustain, and build a business—these are positive, productive emotions that enrich and fuel the enterprise, along with nourishing and empowering the owners. Passion also implies all-out commitment flavored with love, joy, and even anger. When this passion, this excitement, begins to flicker and then die, it is a sign that selling should be in the cards.

In contrast, *anxiety* and *fear*, while sometimes acting as motivators, are mainly negative emotions, which can paralyze, inhibit, or prevent action. In fact, they are warning signs that Freud relates to *danger*. For example, in *Beyond the Pleasure Principle*, Freud distinguishes among what he calls anxiety, fear, and fright. "*Anxiety* describes a particular state of expecting danger or preparing for it, even though it may be unknown." *Fear* requires a "definite object of which to be afraid." And *fright* is "the state of being surprised when danger is unexpected." All three terms can be defined in terms of knowledge, temporality, and expectation. In anxiety, we have some knowledge, although no specific object. (Something is going, on but we don't know what it is.) In fear, we have knowledge and an object for it. (There is a car driving in my lane toward us.) In fright, we have neither knowledge nor an object. (We didn't see the train coming.) Anxiety concerns our expectation regarding the future; fear remembers the past, and fright exists in the present, as a shock or surprise. In a business context, we have concerns about the future of the business, but we are not sure exactly what the concerns are based on. They appear as amorphous thoughts about disruptive technology or the changing competitive landscape and our *ability* to compete. They could be amorphous questions about the talents and interest in the business of the next generation. These thoughts form the basis of *anxiety*.

When the Internet was taking hold as a means of delivering information, print publishers should have had *fear* about the effect *www* would have on their businesses.

Complacent companies have run out of cash, particularly when shareholder distributions exceeded earnings and capital requirements and the well-established companies were not being managed responsibly. As a result, lending sources dry up. When shareholders suddenly stop receiving their regular dividends, the *fright* of running out of cash can be paralyzing.

Both Freud and Jung posited that although fear and anxiety are very physical, their bases were buried in the unconscious. The purpose of psychoanalysis was to bring these emotion-thoughts into consciousness, or awareness. At this point, however, the two analysts differ; all roads for Freud point backward, to infantile sexuality and the Oedipus complex (for men) or the Electra complex (for women)—love for the opposite-sex parent and desire to banish the other. As accurate as the tale of Oedipus may be for male family succession, we are not recommending psychoanalysis as a prerequisite for the selling decision—although at moments, you will think you need it. To simplify, Freud's analysis is focused on self-confidence and the introspective assessment of being able to go to the next level successfully. In my own case, I ultimately realized that I was in competition with my father (and for that matter with my older brother). At the time, this was happening on an intuitive, subconscious level. I had gained tremendous confidence, and I wanted to be better than my dad at his game, and I lost diplomacy in the process, frequently running rough shod over him when I thought I was right and he was wrong.

In my research with families who sold their companies, a significant finding was consistent among all of the family business leaders at the time of their sales. The fear, anxiety, and fright they were experiencing about their companies exceeded the intensity of their passion for continuing to own them. Some were just getting worn out and didn't feel they had the energy or the drive to handle the obstacles that were on the horizon.

Next generation members (exclusive of the leaders), who either worked in the company or didn't and either owned stock in the company or didn't, expressed thoughts concerning ownership that seemed to parallel Carl Jung's work about the individuation process. While many young family members were eager to be identified with and to be involved with the family business, others were concerned about being subsumed by it. They wanted to become their own individual people without carrying the burden of their families' silver spoons. Many were focused on achieving their own self-actualization, perhaps more like a founder than a successor. This was a big part of my neurosis. I wanted to be known for what I created, rather than being known as the boss's son.

Jung's analysis is focused on future opportunities through individuation. In the following example, August Busch III, of the beer company bearing his family name, had an abundance of self-confidence and was driven to become his own man. August Busch IV had neither. August III was a better businessman and company leader—measured by building value of the company and market dominance—than his father was. August III knew in his heart that he could reshape Anheuser Busch to become the leading brewer in the world rather than being locked in head-to-head competition with Schlitz.

A great example of the Oedipus complex playing out in a family company was August Busch III forcing his father, August "Gussie" Busch Jr., out of the leadership of Anheuser Busch Company in 1975 and becoming CEO before he was forty years old. They didn't speak to one another for ten years. His son, August IV, followed his father as CEO of the company, only to lose it in a quasi-hostile takeover less than two years after taking the reins of leadership.

It is immensely important to acknowledge the stranglehold that old, established emotions, particularly fear and anxiety, roiled by new circumstances, can have on our presumed rational decision making. For men, particularly, recognizing and then naming fear and even anxiety are daunting tasks, equated as fear is with cowardice or something equivalently unmasculine.

Jung, on the other hand, explained that these painful effects are singular opportunities for growth, leading to future goals, in a lifelong process that Jung calls individuation. After they are dragged to the surface, these buried thoughts (coloring, cautioning, and even intimidating our actions) can provide clues, if not a road map, for the decision to sell or not. This acknowledgment, while painful, can be a golden opportunity for change. For when acknowledged, fear and anxiety lose their power over us, and we can think and act, clearly.

While identifying with Freud's analysis when I was running the company, I identified with Jung's after selling. I was invited to join a doctoral program and became a university professor. Being only fifty when I sold the company, I had plenty of time to have a second successful career.

To make this process of acknowledgment even more complex, our fears are not only bound up with economic concerns. Family issues, many passed on through the generations, are the source of guilt and shame, along with fear and anxiety. In addition, the sale of a business can be equated with loss of self and identity, failing a family heritage and abandoning future generations.

Here, the Freudian Oedipal tale comes into play, of proper sons identifying with and then replacing their fathers, becoming more successful than their fathers and hence *succeeding* in life or falling below their father's standards and achievements and hence *failing* in business and even in life. Many owners fear that their sons will not want or qualify for the paternal mantle of successor. Sons fear they will fall short of their father's expectations. In the Busch family case, August III became far more successful than his father, and his son, August IV, fell far short of his father's success.

Emotional attachment by family business owner-operators is enormous. The unique cultures of these companies are extensions of the personalities of the founders and their descendants and the extraordinary passion they have for their businesses.

Over time businesses become like family members, and while family members are sometimes disowned, they're never sold. All of the emotional ramifications of severing ties with a loved one come into play.

Personal identity with the company can be incredibly difficult to relinquish. Fear of an unimaginable future without the company is often an obstacle families cannot overcome when considering the possibility of selling.

The idea of selling out their employees—people who have become like family members to them—feels disloyal, even shameful. There is fear and guilt about what the new owners may do to hurt the company, the loyal employees, the suppliers, and the customers who have contributed to its success.

Multishareholder companies present complications in reaching the decision to sell, particularly when factions are formed to advocate various positions for and against selling. The Bancroft family's experience selling Dow Jones & Company, owner of the *Wall Street Journal,* provides a good example. Some of the family members had been disappointed with the company's performance and management for a long time. Others felt strongly about their heritage and legacy; the company could never be sold under any circumstances. The Bancroft family members involved in the governance of the company were against selling, while many of those who were not tended to favor selling.

Competent and well-trained advisors can play a vital role in ferreting out the real reason for selling and facilitating productive discussions among family owners—staying on subject while minimizing the discord that often arises among family members. Bringing an emotionally charged and disparate group to consensus is a job for experts.

When the Oscar Mayer Company was sold, the aging third generation made the decision with little consultation with the fourth generation beneficiaries. Resentments continue to simmer years later among early- and middle-aged fourth-generation members who felt the third generation sold them out, eliminating their opportunity to be involved in the family company and destroying the family legacy.

Several cases with sad endings had a big impact on me. Families lost fortunes as their once successful companies declined and lost their value. The tragic cases were counterbalanced with many happier ones of families who sold their companies. There were new beginnings, philanthropy, and good work free from the burdens and responsibilities of ownership. In many cases the family legacy took on new, enduring meaning and reached an even broader segment of the community at large, freeing family members to self-actualize and individually pursue their own passions and dreams.

Awareness of emotional issues along with the practical issues when considering selling your company is essential in structuring an orderly process that will lead toward an optimal decision for the shareholders.

Not recognizing that selling a family business is a process that must be followed assiduously can result in problems that may diminish the value.

Selling a family business is not an *event*. It's a *process* of the inevitable. Mortality dictates that ultimately ownership will change in every family-owned business in spite of whether or not definitive actions have been taken by the current shareholders.

Recognizing that circumstances, sometimes unforeseen, might dictate a business should be sold to preserve value and being in a state of readiness to sell are the cornerstones of responsible stewardship. In other words, at any given time, an exit plan should be visible to the shareholders. Plans can change when circumstances change. However, top management—the chairman, the CEO, and the CFO—should have a plan for selling the company if it is necessary. Family members at all stages should be aware that a plan exists. Merely having done this work can have a motivating effect on succeeding generations to prepare themselves for leadership roles and demonstrate the passion for becoming involved in the family business.

Consideration of selling begins with the flicker of the first thought all the way through closing the deal and the aftershocks that follow.

Responsible stewardship of family assets takes a long-term view of the financial growth and health of the company. Being prepared to sell the family company under the right conditions doesn't necessarily mean it will ever be sold, but it is an indication of responsible stewardship. Being prepared means the following:

1. Knowing what is happening in the industries your company serves
2. Gauging your family's ability and interest to stay "in the game," including these aspects:
   - Investment capability and debt capacity
   - Management capability
   - Risk tolerance
   - Family and business governance system
   - Family unity
   - Family succession
3. Knowing the value of your company

Sixteen years elapsed from the time the initial thought (a trigger point) crossed my mind about selling our company until it was actually sold. There were several times that I experienced a trigger causing me to pause and sometimes consider the possibility of selling. In my case, more than half of these triggers were external—someone coming to me wanting to purchase our company, either directly or through intermediaries. Others were internal—thinking about mortality and how I was spending my limited time, fear of competition, concerns about the next generation's interest and ability to carry on, or thoughts about monetizing my family's wealth.

Seeing several botched deals made me cautious. There were cases where owners had begun spending the money from the anticipated sale of their companies before they actually closed—only to see the deals fall apart and the buyers walk away.

I also saw cases of business owners losing control of the process of selling their companies. Word leaked out that the company was on the blocks, causing jittery customers and employees to begin defecting. It became imperative that the sellers do a deal—usually at a discount, cents on the dollar—before the company became so damaged that it would be difficult, or worse, impossible to sell.

These experiences made me understand that selling a company is a *complex process* rather than an event. The entire process, culminating in a successful sale, takes time—more time than sellers ever imagine. Buyers are typically involved in multiple transactions, and they follow a disciplined process. The passage of time typically works to their advantage.

When I finally reached the decision to sell, I had closely followed a number of other cases in my own industry and others, and while I knew it would take time—nearly a year or even more to do it right, I had little awareness of how it would unfold. I instinctively knew that when I embarked on the process of selling our company, I would need to follow a disciplined selling process equal to or better than the buyers'. This would be the biggest business deal of my life, and I didn't want to screw it up. Missing, however, was an accurate template I could follow to optimize our outcome and experience.

This book is designed to provide families with a template for exploring, making the decision, and executing the decision to sell their family company. It will also provide insight into life after the family business is sold.

Tired, old companies are harder to sell, and buyers take advantage of a superior negotiating position when buying a company with declining revenue, earnings, and market share. There's an old adage, "When you're green, you're growing; when you're ripe you're rotting." It's far easier to sell a company that appears to have a culture of good results and growth. Companies should regularly be infused with new energy—new talent—to appear as vibrant and well managed.

Top management, owners, and family members should have visibility in their industries and the markets they serve. Anyone can appear as a player in any market just by going to the trade shows, attending industry events, and networking.

Family companies and family members who do not have an experienced, independent board of directors operate at a distinct disadvantage. Positions of management and ownership are very different. The role of the board of directors is to protect the shareholders' ownership interests and to monitor the performance of management. When it comes to evaluating the possible sale of a company, the input and advice provided by board members can provide valuable analysis and recommendations to the shareholders and family members.

History is replete with stories of botched sales. Here are a few of the situations that occurred.

The sellers did not execute a confidentiality agreement. The prospective buyers got into the companies they were allegedly buying under the guise of due diligence. In the process, they were able to examine financial records and learn how the target companies actually operated—including pricing, margins, and costs. Sometimes the prospective buyers learned about products under development. They were able to scavenge for confidential information and use it for competitive reasons. Employees and customers were poached after the prospective buyers terminated discussions and walked away.

Not doing due diligence on buyers often resulted in learning the buyer was unable to consummate a sale because of lack of adequate financial resources. After reaching an agreement, sellers *must* get proof that the buyers have adequate funds to close the deal.

Naïveté and lack of experience have caused many families to make mistakes that reduced the value of their companies, made them nearly impossible to sell, or the deal cratered. Advisers are helpful, if not essential, to helping families think through the process of selling their companies *or parts of their companies.* Experts are essential to leading the sales process to a successful conclusion.

Responsible stewardship suggests the market value of the company and its divisions should be appraised every three years, and in that context, the question should be asked if the current family ownership is best for the business and for the family. Considering the possibility of selling should be evaluated at regular intervals.

In review, the factors constraining families from discussing the possibility of selling include the following:

- It's a taboo topic that shouldn't be brought up.
- Discussions can become emotional.
- There are varying viewpoints among family members—such as whether or not the company should be sold and to whom.
- Participants lack knowledge about selling, even how to intelligently discuss the topic.
- The business family lacks a rational, *systematic process* to evaluate selling.

CHAPTER 3

THE ROAD MAP: EXPLORING AND DECIDING TO SELL

T oo many business owners and families are afraid or unable to explore the possibility of selling their companies. As family businesses grow and develop, the descendants of the founders and business beneficiaries maintain the image—"that's what our family does." They don't think about the company in terms of enterprise value. More typically they relate in terms of products produced, services delivered, income, dividends, allowances, and other unique "owner benefits," such as ski chalets, lake homes, use of private planes, cars, boats, entertainment, vacations, education costs, home maintenance, landscaping, and other services, that only family companies are able to provide family members.

This chapter provides a road map for exploring and making the decision to sell. The next describes the steps to ultimately executing the sale of owner-managed and family companies. *Buyers of these companies are far more experienced in the "art of doing transactions," and their lawyers, accountants, and staff members have gained knowledge and skill through multiple buy/sell/merger deals.* This book is intended to provide guidance and insight, leveling the playing field between first-time sellers and veteran buyers.

In the mid-1990s the academics and consultants in the family business field were singularly focused on helping business families take actions that would enhance their chances to have their companies survive for generations. Their primary metric of success was to increase the percentages of first-generation companies making it through the second generation, second-generation companies making it until the end of the third generation, and so on.

There was plenty of room for improvement, and the academics and consultants looked at their success as helping business families manage their companies and their families through these generational transitions. Many viewed it as a failure when the companies didn't make it—by either going out of business or selling out.

After arriving at the Family Business Center at IMD in Lausanne, Switzerland, in 1996, after our family business was sold, I soon became an outlier in the family business field. I believed that losing a fortune was failure. Period. I was less concerned about how many family businesses had successful transitions to the next generation than I was about the owners of family businesses successfully operating their family businesses and becoming *responsible stewards of their wealth.*

My deep belief meant that there were circumstances that some family businesses needed to be sold in order to protect the families' wealth. I zealously believe there are times when conditions are right to consider the sale of family businesses. There are unique sets of facts and circumstances in every situation. At one time or another, the possibility of selling—remote as it may be—crosses the minds of most family business leaders and family members. Under seemingly identical external circumstances, some families make the decision to sell, and others don't. Sometimes sales are successful; at other times they are not. Exploring the landscape and being informed about the process *never* means that a sale has to be consummated or even that it can be. However, the adage "You can't take it with you" means at some point there must be a disposition— a transaction. It can be a sale, a generational transfer, or an outright gift. As I've said many times, mortality dictates ownership changes. It's just that most of the time, family business owners are not proactive in the process of ownership transfer before their death.

I reiterate, in these rapidly changing and turbulent times, families should be keenly and constantly aware of all the forces and dynamics affecting the industries in which they operate. Technological innovations, globalization, outsourcing, industry consolidation, supplier rationalization, and distribution alternatives are no longer speculation or future possibilities. They're reality.

Every family committed to responsible stewardship of valuable family assets must continually scan the horizon for developments that can impair or potentially destroy the value of their family companies. Some families are threatened by the possibility of selling because they worry that the sale of the family business could mean the end of the family. In reality, the sale of the *family business* can mean the beginning of an exciting new era for the *business family*.

As the CEO of our family-owned business, the magazine-publishing company with periodicals serving more than thirty industries, I had the opportunity to get close-up views of hundreds of family companies during my career. The biggest business tragedies I have witnessed were the demise, bankruptcy, and liquidation of long-established, well-known, and once-respected companies owned by influential families. Pondering those truly sad stories, I always wondered what really happened in those cases and why the families didn't sell when they had the opportunity, rather than presiding over the slow death or burial of a once valuable asset.

I lived in Milwaukee, Wisconsin, and watched the precipitous decline of Schlitz Brewing Company. Schlitz was America's leading brand for years followed by a period of being neck and neck with Budweiser of St. Louis, until CEO Robert Uihlein changed the brewing formula of Schlitz, which began the company's decline, resulting in Budweiser becoming the market leader. Pabst, another Milwaukee brewer, was the nation's largest in the late 1880s. Both family companies were ultimately sold for substantially less money than the families would have received had they sold in their halcyon years.

Unfortunately, not enough business families ever say, "Everything is going so well; maybe we should sell."

To get a vivid and tangible view of businesses that closed their doors, all one has to do is look at old "Main Street" photographs from virtually any town. Dime stores and variety stores that were unable to respond to changing customers and shopping habits as well as new competitors with fresh brands and new ways of doing business were the root causes of failure.

One of the biggest, and saddest, retail transformations was Sears and Roebuck that essentially turned its mail order business over to Amazon and its brick-and-mortar store business over to Walmart. Business history is replete with stories of the companies that simply lost their way and made bad decisions that resulted in their ultimate demise.

Most industrial areas have vacant buildings once occupied by thriving family companies that over time found themselves unable to profitably compete with companies that were better managed, employed new technology, and were able to provide more appealing products at less cost.

Some families overplayed their hands, incurring crushing debt to finance growth or new initiatives that didn't pan out.

There are many stories of family firms that wanted to drive consolidation but didn't have the skill sets to do so and furthermore were hampered by onerous debt service.

The most famous story of wealth dissipation is the Vanderbilt family. Earning their fortune in shipping and railroads and ranked second on the all-time family-wealth list, following the first two generations that included family "wealth creators," excessive spending by succeeding generations squandered the family's enormous holdings, effectively removing their name from the lists of the wealthiest Americans permanently.

Many family business owners who watched their companies lose value for a myriad of reasons simply didn't have the foresight or the courage to exit their businesses while they were doing well and had substantial value.

There are many considerations that go into embarking on a journey to sell the family company. Until the decision is made to either sell or keep the company, there are many questions that arise. In the process, all shareholders and key family members should be interviewed to determine their attitudes about selling.

Confidentiality is of utmost importance so as not to disrupt the operation of the business. If competitors are aware that a company is "in play," they will take advantage of the unsettled situation and swoop in like vultures spreading rumors that can cause irreparable damage.

- Why are we thinking about selling now? What are the triggers?
- What is the value range of the company today?
- Is this the right time to sell?
- What impact will a sale have on the family emotionally and financially?

A big part of the decision will be based on the value of business and how much the financial assets will be able to generate for the benefit of the family after the sale. The key determinants in determining how much the company is worth include the following:

- Current macroeconomic conditions and outlook
- Economic conditions of the industries and markets in which the company operates
- Financial analysis of the company in comparison with other companies in the same or similar business
- Normalization of financial statements (removal of atypical, unusual, and nonrecurring expenditures along with "owner benefits" that the buyer will not have)
- Establishment of a value based on a combination of five approaches:
    1. Income/net earnings over the past four years
    2. Net free cash flow
    3. Asset value
    4. Market comparisons
    5. Future expectations of *potential buyers*

I, together with members of my family, made the decision to sell our family-owned company in 1993. Fascinated by the topic, I subsequently embarked on this study and became a doctoral student and then a professor of entrepreneurship at the University of Wisconsin–Madison and a regular lecturer in the Families in Business program at the Harvard Business School. I have interviewed family business leaders who made the decision to sell their successful companies as well as family business leaders who, after careful consideration, made the decision *not* to sell. Some enjoyed successful continuity, while others saw their companies fail and ultimately go out of business. Others sold at a later date.

After research examining conventional wisdom about why people sell and searching for deeper reasons and motivations, I learned that deciding to sell a family company is not an objective, rational decision. It is rooted deeply in emotion.

That said, there are still more obvious, rational questions that need to be addressed in the decision-making period:

- What are the individual shareholder's objectives?
- Will selling, restructuring, or recapitalizing the company address individual shareholders' objectives and protect family wealth?
- Will the returns on the proceeds of a sale be adequate to meet shareholders' income requirements?
- Is selling or restructuring the ownership of the company the best decision for the owners and the family as responsible stewards of family wealth?

This is the time when "the rubber meets the road" and the shareholders and family determine if they want to continue to carry on the family business, transfer the shares to the next generation or employees, or sell the company to outsiders for the maximum price.

Following is a look at our process of exploring and making the decision to sell our company.

I was very active in our publishing trade association as well as the trade associations in the industries in which we published magazines. I was a student of both successful, well-run companies and those that were failing, and I watched them closely. What fascinated me most was learning about those that were sold and the details of the process they went through. This exploration began shortly after I became CEO of our company starting in 1977.

As our visibility increased in the publishing industry, we regularly received inquiries about our potential interest in selling. At the conclusion of every discussion I had with an investment banker or potential acquirer, I was making a decision about selling or not. Only a couple of the discussions over seventeen years ever gained any traction. Even though these didn't end up going anywhere, the process of talking was a tremendous education for me. Subconsciously I was gradually developing my own templates for exploring the decision to sell and making a decision.

Upon receiving an offer from a Dutch company in 1989, which came at a time when my passion for the business was at a high level, our lead director recommended that we do a dividend strip. I didn't know what this was until he explained it was the same as doing a leveraged buy-out of our own company. To monetize shareholders in 1990, we paid a super dividend totalling half of the appraised value of our company. It amounted to twice our book value and therefore put the company in a negative net worth position. Even so, we were able to borrow the money from a Milwaukee bank without any personal guarantees, although the assets of the company were pledged as collateral. The dividend provided liquidity and a feeling of financial security for our family members while we still owned the company.

In my own case, I had fear. My father had a few business failures of which I was well aware. Shortly after recapitalizing our company, we surprisingly and unexpectedly lost over 40 percent of our business in our most profitable division. While still profitable, I worried about losing more business, about our ability to service our debt, and about losing the wealth I had worked so hard to build up. People were just starting to talk about the Internet and the possibilities it offered to do an infinite number of undefined tasks. I had anxiety about the impact it could have on our business—print publications. In short, I was scared, and it was taking a toll on me. I felt like I was between a rock and a hard place. However, change came fast. And on a positive note, I learned a great deal about operating a highly leveraged company.

The business needed to be fixed, and it was going to take four years to restore a track record of growth. I was determined to make the company stronger that it ever was—together with our key people and a few new hires, following the termination of some high paid people who had been, in my judgment, too opportunistic about getting new business. The business they brought in didn't have a lasting quality, and it didn't fit with our definition of ideal customers. Those executives were difficult to manage, and in the end, it was tough to bring them into alignment with our vision and processes, which they viewed as cumbersome, while they were enjoying short-term success. They were spoiled by our incentive compensation system that favored the short term, so with the benefit of hindsight, we did it to ourselves.

In less than four years, we had restored the health of our company. We had record sales, profits, *no debt*, and large cash reserves. The company had nearly taken on the characteristics of a lucrative annuity. In short, I was settling in for the long haul and was hopeful that my daughter, Amy, would join the company and become my successor. She had done very well working in our internship program and enjoyed tremendous popularity among the people at the company. I thought that after a few years getting experience working in New York, she could return to our company in a responsible job and become my successor when she was ready. It was no time to seriously consider selling, although there continued to be interest from prospective acquirers.

Early in this euphoric period as our company was again enjoying success and gaining momentum, I received a call from my daughter. She asked me to meet her for dinner in New York where she was working in the advertising business. Over our first drink, she said, "Dad, I believe publishing is my destiny but not my passion. Maybe I would feel somewhat different if you published fashion magazines in a major city rather than agricultural and distribution magazines in a rural town in Wisconsin. I want to go back to school and get a degree in education and become a teacher. That's what I'm passionate about." It was a bittersweet conversation. I was proud of how she was developing as a strong woman and adult, but I was deeply disappointed in her changed career plan.

Two years later, I received an unsolicited call from the investment banker for a company that had paid generously for one of our magazines that didn't fit our portfolio strategy a few years earlier. Two venture capital companies had owned them for seven years, and the owners were anxious for a liquidity event. The venture capital partners thought their investment was languishing, and they needed to be able to make a significant acquisition to make their company more attractive so it could be more readily sold. Our company had nearly the same revenue as the potential acquirer, but our company was more profitable.

Realizing what our company was worth at the time, I began thinking there was no euphoria I could ever experience by making it worth more that would offset the despair I would feel if it was ever worth less. It made compelling sense to sell; however, it was fear, anxiety, and even fright that drove me, reinforced by my diminishing passion for the business. In retrospect, I learned that it's critical that there's a ready buyer when a company is ready to sell. In my case, the stars lined up.

When I recognized that the optimum decision for our family was to sell, I felt I had incredibly sound, objective reasons for doing so. But I fully understand now, that I created the rational explanation to support my gut feelings. I don't want to imply that objective analysis and reasoning don't play a part in the decision, because they do—a big part. I just want to emphasize that the real reasons are rooted in emotion rather than rationale. It was a case of my losing passion for the business, especially knowing that my daughter was not interested in being a part of it. This was coupled with the fear I had of our company losing value like my dad's previous experiences...and I was feeling growing anxiety about the possible threat of the Internet

Conventional Wisdom

Selling hasn't gotten much attention from universities with family business courses and programs, and there has been very little in-depth research on the topic. Conventional wisdom attributed selling to poor performance, lack of management successors, getting an offer that "could not be turned down," and other rather superficial reasons. This has been changing in recent years.

John Davis, chair of Harvard Business School's Families in Business program, is speaking and writing more frequently about selling the family business. In his article, "The Five Derailers of Effective Succession," he directly mentions selling when there is no one in the family who is both interested and qualified to lead the business. This dialogue has increased among other leading family business scholars who in the past seldom even alluded to selling.

They historically viewed the inability to successfully pass ownership from generation to generation as a failure of sorts. And their mission was to help families make their businesses sustainable over generations.

While lack of qualified successors may be triggers for considering the possibility of selling, there are many successful family companies that choose to ameliorate those challenges. Their companies are now being managed and led by top-level nonfamily executives. Some have gone public to create liquidity for the family members and key executives, but they have two classes of stock—one of which allows the families to maintain "control" even though majority ownership is in the hands of public shareholders. (August Busch III never did that, making Anheuser Busch ultimately vulnerable to a takeover.)

Selling founder-owned and family companies encompasses far more complex issues—like moral considerations and philosophical predispositions. In strictly public or investor-owned companies, in contrast to family-controlled public or investor-owned companies, selling boils down to business and financial implications related to increasing shareholder value.

It was easy to organize reasons for selling businesses (the *trigger points*) into the categories of the Three-Circle Model discussed in the first chapter—Business, Family, and Ownership. These triggers should stimulate exploration to assure that *uninformed* decisions are *not* being made.

Business Reasons for Selling:

- Changing industry dynamics making it difficult to complete
- Industry consolidation
- Lack of growth opportunities
- Need to change core business
- Weak economy
- Restrictive environmental changes
- Sick industry with poor outlook
- Shrinking market
- Business too demanding
- New global competition
- Disruptive technology
- Losing market share
- Debilitating price wars
- Eroding profitability
- Capital requirements
- Reduced appetite for risk
- Protection against an uncertain future with the company
- Tax issues that encourage a sale now
- Soaring valuations and high purchase prices

- Product liability exposure
- Increasing litigious activity in the industry
- Government regulation and constraints
- Management relations problems
- Lack of successor management prospects
- High employee turnover
- Inability to attract talent
- Changing skill set requirements in the company
- Owners losing interest in and passion for the business
- Emergence of the "perfect" buyer
- Aging management
- Need for new blood and energy in the business

Family Reasons for Selling:

- Conflict in the family and unrest
- Low family morale and interest in keeping the company
- Backbiting and negative intrigue
- Divorce
- Stress on marital and family relationships
- Poor prognosis for family relationships
- Company not compatible with family values or supporting family's image
- Differing interests of active and passive owners
- Liberating children from a "duty millstone"
- No passion in the family for the business
- Income security and liquidity for family/shareholders
- Estate planning needs
- Fear of business failure
- Benefits of diversification of family wealth
- Poor financial returns to shareholders
- Market value of the company exceeds earning ability of the company
- No talent in the family to carry on the company as leaders or responsible shareholders

Ownership Reasons for Selling:

- Getting an unsolicited offer that cannot be prudently refused
- Age of owners active in the business
- Lack of interested younger generation
- Burned out—no more appetite to fight the competitive battles
- Fed up with employees, relatives and the business
- Physically worn out and tired
- Desire to monetize wealth and be relieved of responsibility
- Tax issue encouraging a sale
- Insufficient liquidity
- Less appetite for risk, leverage, and loan guarantees
- Desire to retire and leave the business
- Join friends who have sold their companies
- Desire to do other things
- To have complete independence outside of the business

Very different outcomes among companies in virtually identical external circumstances reveal that conventional wisdom doesn't fully explain the decision to sell. There is more to why some companies make the decision to sell and others don't.

Critical Determinants

The real answers to why some companies sell and others don't can be spelled out by the juxtaposition of passion for the business and company versus fear, fright, and anxiety.

- *Passion: ardent affection, a strong liking for or devotion to some activity*
- *Fear: an unpleasant emotional state characterized by anticipation of pain or great distress*
- *Fright: the state of being surprised when danger is unexpected*
- *Anxiety: a state of being anxious or of experiencing a strong or dominating blend of uncertainty, agitation, or dread and brooding fear about some contingency.*

My father had business reverses and lost everything he and my grand-father had accumulated early in his career. When he was in his sixties, after a brief period of retirement, he developed another company on which he bet most of his net worth. Unfortunately, it was not successful, and he finally had to dispose of the assets in a distressed sale and carry the remaining debt of bank loans he had personally guaranteed. While I helped him retire his debt so he could have a secure retirement, I feared the possibility of history repeating itself and was afraid of the way I would feel if I rejected a great offer for the company, never to receive another so lucrative.

Every family business leader experiences both fear and anxiety about the business at various times. These feelings can be motivating or debili-tating, but when their intensity *exceeds* the intensity of the family's pas-sion for the business and the company, it's time to sell. When the passion is dying, bad things begin to happen—loss of the innovative spirit and soul that drives the business; loss of market share; decaying business pro-cesses; aging and, in some cases, obsolete plant and equipment; dete-riorating employee morale; and erosion of financial performance and liquidity. It's extremely difficult to reverse the direction.

In my case, when the intensity of my fear about possible financial reverses and anxiety about the Internet exceeded the intensity of my passion and my family's passion for the business and the company, I realized it was prudent for us to sell. At the time my gut feelings rather than a deep understanding of motivations propelled me. However, my inherent value orientation made the risks to the business appear more ominous than perhaps they really were at the time.

It wasn't until my passion for the business was dying that I was able to look at the personal issues impacting my decision. It was still the most difficult decision of my life. The professionals, investment bankers, lawyers, accountants, financial advisors, and board members, who are involved as advisors on business sale transactions, generally overlook the intersection of emotion and practicality.

We consummated a successful sale of the company, and the next generation was free and unencumbered to pursue their own pas-sions with intensity, focus, and enthusiasm. As Carl Jung explains, the next generation members of the family business were able to work toward their own individuation—as I was at age fifty. The relationship between the intensity of fear and anxiety and the intensity of passion for the business and the company has played out as the critical decision-making determinant of whether or not to sell in every case I have studied.

There was more exploration before we began executing the process. We continued the exploration process so we could become better informed to make such an important decision. And when we finally made it, there was a lot involved in developing the optimal strategy.

Exploration Process

During the exploration process, following are the things that should be done to enhance all family members' understanding of the business and the company before any decision making begins regarding a possible liquidity event.

- A reputable and independent firm that has experience in the industry should prepare a valuation of the company. This will answer the question about the value range of the company. This is usually a key factor in making a decision to either continue exploring a possible sale or abandoning the endeavor, at least until the valuation changes.

- For those adult family members who don't really have a sense of the company and its industry position, it's helpful to attend industry trade shows and industry conventions and disclose your relationship with the company during these exploratory visits; just try to learn about the dynamics and economics of the industry.

- If a company in your industry sold recently, it is interesting to find out as much as you can about the sale, including the price and the process the selling company went through. It's usually a cathartic experience for people who have sold their companies to share their story.

- Interview and gather information about every shareholder's and family member's attachment to the company and their wishes to be involved as employees and responsible owners now and in the future. Try to ascertain their timelines for involvement.

- Have get acquainted meetings with the best known and respected investment bankers and brokers in the industry to both get a sense of them as well as to get insight about the market—its current situation and future prospects for both buying and selling.
- Meet with family members from companies who have gone through the process of selling out in order to learn about their experiences.
- Speak with board members and company advisors associated with companies that have sold to get the benefit of their experiences and wisdom.
- Try to meet with other family business owners, not in your industry, to get their perspectives about the experience of selling their own companies. They are generally forthcoming about sharing with people who are in situations similar to theirs.

If your own company is showing the signs of deterioration, corrective action should be taken. The infusion of new talent can be a tremendous asset in revitalizing a company in need of improved performance.

An informed decision really can't be made about selling until the infusion of new energy starts to pay off.

It's easy to be a player in any market. Maintain openness to creating relationships—whether it's forming alliances and partnerships or making acquisitions that are strategically aligned with your core business. *The appearance of being a buyer in the market is extraordinarily educational.* Seeing inside information on other companies provides an opportunity to assess your own performance and to benchmark it against others. As a buyer, you can see information about other companies that are planning to sell and see their selling materials and financial records.

If and when you are ready to be a seller, you can make a quiet, discreet transition from being a buyer to becoming a seller. While it can be a subtle step, you will know the lay of the land—the key companies in your market as well as performance metrics. You will have compelling insight that will be invaluable during the selling process. And you will be able to camouflage your position as a seller during the exploration period, because, after all, there is a sense that you're already in the market and open to opportunities that can be best for the business, the family, and the owners. There is no such thing as gathering too much information when approaching a potential sale of your family business.

The exploration phase of selling has no time limit. In fact, in my case it spanned years, and I just kept learning during that period. It was *not* a waste of time.

At the outset, an initial trigger gets the ball rolling. Usually it's an unsolicited call out of the blue from a prospective buyer or their representative; a disruptive change in the marketplace that may potentially damage the company; a health problem or an untimely death; a family feud; or a friend or acquaintance who "hit the jackpot" with a successful sale. The list is long.

All kinds of amorphous thoughts follow these initial trigger points. They are wide, varied, and confusing. It's impossible to anticipate or think about all the ramifications often leading to gridlock or, worse yet, bad decisions.

Every trigger and amorphous thought about selling can be classified as one of three: personal feelings about continuing ownership, business issues, or family considerations.

If there is bona fide interest in pursuing the idea of selling, financial statements and company performance should be scrutinized and the estimated value of the company can begin to be established. If it seems to be adequate, *it's time for a decision point.*

"If we were to sell, how much could we realistically get?" An actual, verifiable business valuation is required if considerations of selling are to continue. Frequently sellers are overly optimistic of the value of their companies only to be disappointed after spending a great deal of time and effort pursuing a sale. When a realistic price for the company is inadequate—it's time to regroup and consider options.

Usually, the family realizes that decisions have to be made and actions have to be taken to increase the value of the company before going to market.

In every business segment, it is relatively easy to learn comparable values—almost like real estate. Accountants, lawyers, brokers, and investment bankers can readily come up with pretty reliable estimates of value based on previous sales of similar companies (*without spending a significant amount of time or money*). It's wise to get value estimates from a variety of sources to get a reality check. Invariably, there are extremes on both the low and high side. Investigation of the rationale for all estimated valuations will prove helpful in positioning the company and finding the best prospective buyers.

Going through repetitive cycles of "to sell or not to sell" is typical of most family business owners. The road map (Appendix A) highlights the cyclic nature of the exploration period, which has helped sellers organize their thinking and learn more each time it occurs.

During the exploration period, it is useful for the key decision makers to have independent sounding boards to supplement and test their thinking. Influencers may be friends, relatives, or acquaintances who have had experience or may know something about selling companies. Beginning in the early stage of the exploration period, influencers play a significant role having conversations and raising questions with family business leaders about the possibility of selling. Influencers should be the first people family business leaders talk to about the possibility of selling. They are individuals the family leaders respect and like and with whom they feel comfortable.

The dialogue with influencers continues through the entire process until the family business owners either consummate a sale, decide to abort the process, or the deal falls apart. Influencer relationships tend to have permanence; however, it's important to recognize that influencers can have shelf lives. When influencers fall away, they should be replaced. As people and companies go through evolutions, the experience of a particular influencer can become irrelevant. There is no evidence that any family business leaders went through the selling process without confiding in multiple influencers and brainstorming about business issues, family considerations, and ownership concerns.

The group of influencers (consulted individually to avoid "groupthink") can include advisors, like the company lawyer and outside accountant and possibly members of the board. It should be emphasized these discussions at the outset are early stage and should appear to be informal, just information gathering. However, to give structure to the conversations, discussions should revolve around business issues, family considerations, the approximate market value of the company, and personal feelings about continued ownership. This will lead to a more informed decision point each time selling the company or a portion of it is considered.

Following unrushed and thoughtful initial conversations with influencers, an answer is bound to emerge over time. "No, not now, or maybe some time in the future" are conclusions that return the decision makers to a commitment to company ownership, at least for the present time. If the answer is yes, it's a good idea to sell and a good time to sell; the conversations with influencers will become deeper, more meaningful, and more formal and will lead to a considered decision about selling or not at this decision point. If the answer is no, the narrative returns to a commitment to company ownership.

Critical to responsible ownership is maintaining awareness of the value of the enterprise and how best to protect it. This suggests prudent owners should always be in some state of readiness—that if an unexpected, exceptionally positive, or untoward event (trigger point) occurs, the notion of an exit plan exists. In too many cases, a trigger point forces a decision to sell without having explored and being prepared for the ultimate possibility of selling. Precipitous transactions can result in a significant diminution of value.

Some enlightened owners and leaders are alert to exit possibilities through continual engagement in an exploratory process. This is a safe, nonthreatening, prudent, and worthwhile educational exercise that has the potential of paying huge dividends. An ideal way to approach this process is to always be, at the very least, on the fringe of the Merger and Acquisition market. Being a potential acquirer or joint venture partner is a good way to gain information without being a seller.

Assuming this posture allows family business leaders get the "lay of the land," and they go through many of the amorphous thoughts related to ownership concerns, family considerations, business issues, and the value of their companies. Initial discussions with confidants and the advice and counsel that are obtained from them are part of this initial period.

An analysis of whether the financial outcome of selling now appears to be superior or not necessarily more lucrative to the perceived present and future financial benefits of owning the company—the decision to either stop or proceed with the exploration process—is relatively easy. Risk should be taken into account. If the decision is not to sell and to continue, the hard work begins. Merely going through this process can reenergize owners to consider the value of their companies and make the decisions to improve performance and make it grow.

If thorough consultation with influencers results in an inclination to move forward toward a sale, the next step is consultation with key stakeholders. These conversations should take place one-on-one, avoiding the possibility of "groupthink" or allowing anyone to hijack the process. It may be helpful and important to have an unbiased, trusted friend or advisor to the family participate in these discussions to ameliorate emotion and the possibility of getting off track. Serious preparation should be done before each of these meetings.

The exploration period fades, and for families who become interested in the idea of selling, the decision-making period advances. When momentum is gaining traction in favor of selling the company and a choice between pursuing a sale or recommitting to company ownership is becoming clear, it's time to begin getting the stakeholders on the same page—while still being able to turn back.

Don't think it's easy to back out of the process once you've made the decision to sell and engage the process. It quickly becomes a one-way ticket.

Once the decision to sell is made, the sellers often begin to focus on what they're moving toward rather than what they're moving from. That's a big mistake. Selling a company takes time; it's complicated, and a myriad of things can go wrong. Vigilance and laser-like attention to all the details are essential.

Prospective buyers are anxious for sellers to become detached and look ahead rather than paying careful attention to the present. The passage of time works to the advantage of buyers rather than sellers. Buyers want to control the process—entice the owners to sell and have an agreement in principle in place subject to due diligence—and then have a protracted due diligence period to search for things that are wrong or, at least, not exactly as represented. The objective is to learn things that might undermine or diminish the agreed upon value of the company. They are also looking for potentially big issues they didn't anticipate that might make them walk away from the deal altogether. And, at the very least, buyers work hard to make discoveries during due diligence that will lower the final amount they have to pay from the initial offer.

As time passes, word about the impending transaction can become known, and it becomes more and more difficult to control the process and retreat without severe damage to the company and the trust of the employees and other stakeholders.

Exploration of the possibility of selling was over when our family (and all the others I studied) resolutely reached the decision to proceed with selling the family business after carefully considering all of the attendant facts.

Decision-Making Period

It's important to mention that the decision to sell does not need to include the whole company. Parts of it may be sold, and those parts—subsidiaries, divisions, facilities, product lines, technology, and intellectual property—may generate substantial returns to the owners. The units that are sold may not be strategically aligned with a future streamlined or re-formed company, and selling them will not only generate funds, but it also may even increase the value of the remaining company because of its sharper focus. The exploration and decision-making process are the same for selling parts or the entire company. And if the family sells only a part, they will still have a remaining company to own and manage.

So much of the decision-making process depends on the ownership constellation of the company—whether the shares are controlled by a single individual, a group of siblings, cousins, or a mix of family members from different generations. There is a myriad of ownership combinations that can make the selling process very complicated. In addition, the development stages of both the business and the owning family have an impact on the decision-making process. Each ownership structure has unique characteristics.

Trusted advisors and influencers play a vital role in the decision-making process by providing an independent and objective voice in the deliberations. Their role is particularly critical in complicated ownership constellations where they are able to keep discussions on track and minimize emotional diatribes.

Thorough discussions with influencers about the possibility of selling typically address various outcomes and their impact on the owners and their families. They may include financial considerations, the types of potential buyers, and subsequent effects on the company and its people. These discussions tend to influence the next steps the family owners will take and therefore mark the beginning of the decision-making period.

It is wise to have a current, up-to-date estate plan *before* making the final decision to sell. Not doing so can be a very costly mistake.

Young and middle-aged people seldom think about death and therefore don't make the requisite financial plans for that eventuality. Sometimes older people don't as well. If you want to minimize taxes associated with financial wealth, it is *never* too early to begin planning.

Hire experienced professionals to guide you through the necessary steps to maximize the value of your estate when it is transferred to succeeding generations. And don't procrastinate. It doesn't matter how small or how large your estate is now; waiting to prepare your plan will cost money—lots of it. Families who have a current plan taking into consideration the latest tax regulations do so much better.

Responsible ownership dictates that planning for the range of options associated with the ultimate ownership transition is addressed. This should be a topic of regular review, and a plan should always be in place to accommodate unforeseen circumstances. For sure, these plans can and will change over time.

There is flexibility in the valuation of closely held businesses, and transactions can be structured in ways to decrease the impact of taxes on both buyers and sellers. This flexibility disappears when passing assets with clear, unambiguous market values to succeeding generations. It's never too early to start the process of planning for the inevitable ownership transfer. Many options and combinations are available for transferring ownership; however, the greatest benefits of careful estate planning inure to those who do it early rather than at the last possible minute. In my own case, my advisors and I began twelve years before the sale.

Companies that have been successfully passed from generation to generation have been beneficiaries of solid, effective work in this area. Also, families who wish to keep their wealth in the family—regardless of the ultimate disposition of the company—will also benefit greatly from professional estate planning. "Selling" or gifting stock directly to beneficiaries or trusts before significant value appreciation can significantly reduce the ultimate tax burden.

It's hard to understand why business owners procrastinate in dealing with this important issue. It's axiomatic that there's nearly a linear relationship between the ultimate tax bill on wealth transfer and the length of time the owners procrastinate in making transfers to family members or trusts for their beneficiaries.

In the course of discussions with influencers, the family business leaders will make a decision to either stop thinking about selling or to keep an open mind about the process. To this point, conversations sharing knowledge, experience, and insight have contributed to organizing thoughts through examination of various factors to be considered.

If, for whatever reason or combination of reasons, a negative decision is reached, consideration of selling ends. The owners should commit themselves to continued leadership and development of the family company. The reasons for discontinuing the exploration process may be temporal and therefore should never be considered permanent or final. Facts and circumstances can change at any moment.

When family business leaders make decisions to stop exploring the possible sale of their companies, they've made the commitment to continued ownership consciously or not. Often, through the process of examining alternatives, the idea of owning and operating a family company takes on new life. It can have a very positive effect. During the exploratory process, family business leaders see other companies and their relative market value and in turn look at their own companies in a different light. Seeing the family company from a new perspective can be a broadening experience; ideas can develop that will provide enhancements and improvements that contribute to increasing the company's value over time.

Once family business leaders have explored the possibility of selling—even on a preliminary, superficial basis—they will be more vulnerable to future trigger points than ever before, and they will occur. Depending on the circumstances surrounding the family business at the time, subsequent triggers may start the process again. Ownership concerns dominate, and if the family business leaders are unwilling to consider selling, they won't, unless a majority of owners feel otherwise and force discussions to take place. When consideration of selling reoccurs, increasingly earnest explorations of selling resume, and greater involvement in the decision-making process becomes evident.

Families typically go through the consideration cycle numerous times spanning several years. Each cycle of examining their business issues, family considerations, ownership concerns, and the value of their companies can be a tremendous learning experience. The family business leaders become more introspective, and they realize that if and when the right time for them to sell their companies comes along, they will be more likely to recognize it. As they fill their metaphorical file folders with data—objective information and emotional feelings—they understand themselves and those around them much better.

Family business leaders who understand themselves, their families, their companies, their industries, and the value of their companies tend to execute more successful transactions. They respond to repetitive trigger points and go through the process until all, or a significant number, of the arguments for selling are in alignment. In their minds this repetitive experience develops intuition and prepares them to seize the opportunity at precisely the right moment. For those family business leaders, the process may take on the profile of a grand strategic plan.

The more experience family business leaders have considering and exploring the possibility of selling, the better equipped they feel they are to effectively decide which trigger points warrant response. The phenomenon of repetitive cycles and related exposure to the selling process bolsters the family business leaders' confidence to lead the selling process.

When the decision is made *not* to proceed with the selling process, passionate recommitment to ownership of the company hopefully takes place. It can be easy if withdrawal is by choice, or difficult if mandated by circumstances beyond the owner's control. In both cases, however, those involved have learned more and can incorporate new ideas and knowledge into the operation of the business. Typically, the value of the enterprise increases after recommitment to company ownership, because the family business leaders have a better understanding of the components that contribute to increasing the value of their businesses (that may be sold later).

The final step during the decision-making process involves consultation with key stakeholders. They include the other shareholders and family members. The circle gradually widens on a "need to know" basis. Key employees and professional service providers may be included. Generally, family business leaders will not consult with key stakeholders until the idea of selling is really fixed in their minds for fear of causing unnecessary disruption to the company and the family. When family business owners have, in fact, made the decision to sell with counsel from influencers, subsequent consultation with other shareholders and stakeholders could appear perfunctory and superficial. Therefore, these sensitive conversations demand diplomacy and extraordinary professionalism. It may be wise to include "high-status" and respected influencers in these discussions.

Typically, the consultation with key stakeholders at this late stage is "a presentation of the decision" that the family business leader has, in fact, already made. It generally includes a recitation of the business issues, family considerations, and outcome for the owners with an objective to build consensus for the decision.

Agreement among family members may never happen, although alignment might. Getting on the same page is critical before the execution process begins in order to have a successful sale. There are things that can be done to ameliorate varying interests. Family business and financial advisors are particularly well suited to accomplish this. Alternatives regarding ownership constellations—recapitalizing, raising debt, bringing in new shareholders, or investment in new ventures—can be explored. The end of the family business as a result of selling does not have to mean the end of the business family. Monetizing family wealth offers many possibilities and can be discussed positively with the help of advisors.

When the owners are in alignment, the process proceeds to the execution period. This also will be the case if a dissident segment (minority) of the ownership group or family members disagree. Majority ownership will ultimately win out. If fresh thinking can be provided bringing a better idea of how to proceed, the process may be derailed or the course may be changed with the advice and consent of the leaders and majority shareholders.

Kenny Rogers advises:

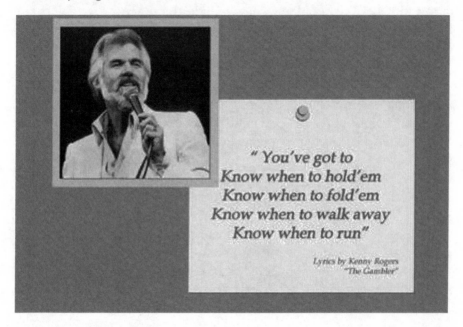

" You've got to
Know when to hold'em
Know when to fold'em
Know when to walk away
Know when to run"

Lyrics by Kenny Rogers
"The Gambler"

CHAPTER 4

EXECUTING THE DECISION TO SELL

There is no confidentiality. So, don't begin executing unless there's certainty there will be a buyer at a price the shareholders will accept.

In spite of confidentiality agreements or what the investment bankers or potential buyers may say about confidentiality, understand at the outset there is none. Typically, a "black book" or offering memorandum is prepared that fully describes the company— (served markets, products, market share data, product line profitability, manufacturing processes, supply chain and distribution information, key personnel, and much more)—being offered for sale, including complete financial information for the past several years in addition to projections for the future. Prospective buyers primarily use this information to make their valuation and acquisition decisions. This information typically gets wide distribution within each prospective buyer's company. The distribution of this "confidential material" includes internal people as well as external advisors. And every prospective buyer's entire team can be exposed to *all* the information about the subject company. It's naïve to think otherwise. The thought that this information can remain confidential is a myth. That's why it is imperative that sellers are sure they want to sell when the ball gets rolling because the process is difficult to stop once it's started.

The inner circle at the selling company should be small and remain small throughout the process—limited only to those employees who truly have a "need to know." Critical employees should be offered "stay or retention bonuses" to incentivize them to remain with the company.

It can be very damaging to begin a selling process and not be able to complete it for lack of a buyer. Sellers should have certainty before starting—certainty that there will be ready buyers for the company at a price acceptable to shareholders. When these conditions are met, confidentiality is less important.

Don't try to fix the business *while* you're trying to sell it. Be ready before you go to market. When things are *not* going well at the company, it's no time to sell. Get it fixed first.

A critical step in the process of selling a company is to engrave the Boy Scout's motto, "*Be Prepared*," into the psyche of every member of the selling team. It should be enough to know that astute buyers are trained to look for problems during the due diligence process—problems that will either reduce the price at closing or require large reserves to be placed in escrow for a period of time after completion of the sale. Simply stated, the company needs to be ready to be sold.

The financial statements need to be scrubbed—special charges and "excess owner benefit expenses" need to be identified and removed from the pro forma statements. Those costs will be eliminated immediately after the buyer pays up and the deal is closed. Losing ventures, product lines, and operations that are averse to the profitability and health of the company must be eliminated. Unproductive employees should be terminated—given early retirement or generous severance packages to leave if that's necessary.

Chances are if there are problems in the company, they'll be discovered during the selling process. Count on it!

After the sale is closed, the new owners will begin cutting unnecessary expenses and getting rid of unprofitable activities to increase earnings and recapture as much of the purchase price as quickly as possible. This is the first thing astute buyers do after taking control of their acquisitions.

Cleaning up the company before selling means that the value of the profit improvements will inure to the seller's benefit rather than the buyer's.

Make sure customer relationships are secure. If price increases are possible, institute them before the sale. Anything that can be done to improve the annual profitability of the business will come back multifold in the purchase price.

Dying passion and ownership fatigue can cause sellers to overlook or discard the important task of getting the company *ready for sale*. And it's imperative this work be done before going to market.

Your old advisors—lawyer(s) and accountant(s)—may not be up to the job and may not have the requisite experience to go toe to toe with experienced buyers and their legal teams. One of the biggest mistakes sellers make is born out of loyalty—loyalty to the professionals who have been in faithful service to the company over the years. Lawyers, accountants, intermediaries, and financial advisors who are not steeped in merger and acquisition experience are the wrong people to handle this complex process. Most buyers have done multiple deals, and they have teams of experts who do nothing but put deals together. Advisors who are *not* specialists in this activity are outmatched by those professionals who are. It's important to put together the best possible team of experts to represent you—the seller—in negotiating and executing a deal to sell your company. This doesn't preclude involvement of your traditional advisors, who, of course, can be participants, but they should not be leading the process and going toe to toe with the experts on the buyer's side.

Family advisors who have had long-standing relationships with families and their companies can certainly add value. They can be extraordinarily helpful in facilitating family dynamics in order to achieve alignment and consensus.

Remember, most sellers do one big deal in their careers—and for buyers, making acquisitions is part of their regular routine. It's not smart to enter the process with a lopsided playing field in terms of experience. Assemble the best possible team you can. This is no time for on-the-job training.

I am a believer in using experienced, reputable investment bankers (particularly those experienced in selling similar companies in the same or related industries) to advise owners on the sale of their companies. The list of positive reasons is long and compelling.

These professionals have encyclopedic knowledge about comparable transactions, actual valuations, active buyers, and the execution process—all the way to the ultimate wire transfer of funds coincident with closing the deal. They are also able to effectively create the illusion of an auction or a bevy of competitive buyers even when there is none.

And good, professional investment bankers should be able to run a disciplined selling process.

Buyers generally prefer to work with intermediaries. There are several reasons. First, a seller who has engaged an investment banker is demonstrating seriousness and commitment to selling. Dealing with a professional intermediary minimizes the potential for emotionally charged encounters (which can derail a deal) during the negotiating process. Using an investment banker can go a long way toward keeping the selling process on track—it puts starch in the process—and the reality that investment bankers get paid for consummating transactions suggests they are not prone to waste time with endless negotiations that can be detrimental to a successful outcome.

The first revealing misunderstanding is that after the engagement of the investment banker, it soon becomes apparent that the investment banker has shifted and seems to be working harder for the buyers than for the seller. Questions of loyalty, even betrayal, begin to emerge. While the investment banker has become the seller's newest best friend during the courtship phase, once the engagement letter is signed there is a seismic shift.

At the outset, it should be obvious to sellers this change will occur because there will be no transaction unless a buyer actually comes forward and is willing to meet the demands of the seller. The investment banker must shift emphasis at some point and at best, reach compromise or, at worst, simply be focused on convincing the seller to accept the buyer's terms and conditions. This can be a rude awakening for the seller who has placed extraordinary confidence in the investment banker to fight the battle for a successful outcome on the sellers' terms rather than the buyers'.

Investment bankers are busy—often working on numerous deals simultaneously and trying hard to close them as quickly and efficiently as possible. It's a given that details can be overlooked or ignored. Therefore, sellers should have laser-like, single-minded focus on remaining engaged in overseeing the work of their investment bankers during the selling process, particularly during the preparation phase.

It can also become disheartening to learn that the investment banker is neglecting nuances of value about the company in their selling effort.

That's why it's important for the principals of the selling company to stay close to the process and continue to work closely with bankers on fine-tuning the message.

Frequently, bankers will cajole sellers into accepting conditions that are represented as typical and customary. There is no requirement that sellers accept the so-called typical and customary conditions. In fact, the stronger the seller's position and the more desire the buyer has for concluding the sale, the more everything is on the table for negotiation and the seller can have more leverage than might be apparent. That's the benefit of sellers' doing complete work on learning about the buyer and all their reasons for wanting to buy the company. If their reasons are compelling, the buyers will not want to blow the deal at the eleventh hour by being arbitrary.

It's customary that after the seller accepts the initial letter of intent—the remaining work is confined to the "winning bidder." This is when the buyer gets the edge...and tries to take control of the process in terms of time and conditions.

It's no wonder sellers want to slip into nirvana and begin investing yet to be gotten cash into their new "postsale retirement" lifestyle. The most disastrous cases I've seen occur when the sellers actually begin spending the money and making investments from the proceeds of the sale before the deal is done. If the sale collapses, what happens next will be a cascade of horrendous problems. And it's very tough to regenerate enthusiasm for owning the business after the process of "letting go" has commenced.

The execution period is the unforgiving period when every *t* must be crossed and every *i* must be dotted. Either "selling fatigue" or "anticipated liquidity exhilaration" can easily take the seller's eye off the ball. This is a huge mistake. Executing the sale of their company is the biggest deal most sellers will make in their lifetime. And it's not an internal activity; it's an external activity. It is, in fact, a competitive sport—between a seller and a buyer, each trying to better the other.

Many things can go wrong during the execution process, and if the seller is not fully engaged to keep the process on course, a sale may not be consummated, and all the unfulfilled expectations will create another set of emotionally vexing problems.

This appeared to be happening in the process of selling our company. I grew very frustrated as closing dates were delayed, and more and more inane requests for information and access came from the buyers. They were wearing me out, and I began to feel tremendous anxiety about whether our sale would be concluded on the agreed upon terms and even if it would happen at all. I became suspicious that our investment bankers were complicit in the delaying tactics, when they merely explained to me time after time that these delays just happen and there's really nothing that can be done about them.

As the supposed closing dates came and went, I realized there was far less "push back" from the investment bankers. They became little more than messengers but with accompanying instructions to comply with the requests of the buyer in order to move toward a conclusion. It no longer felt like we had any control of the process.

Finally, it should be obvious to sellers that they are providing investment bankers "one shot" opportunities. When the deal is closed, the bankers collect their fees and move on. On the other hand, buyers can provide an annuity to the bankers through multiple transactions if the buyers perceive the banker is doing a good job for them. Buyers remain important players in the game—as acquirers, merger candidates, or even future sellers. It's understandable and just good business for investment bankers to conduct themselves in a way that impresses the buyers and builds a solid foundation for future transactions. Unfortunately, I was oblivious to this dynamic. I wish I had been able to anticipate and ameliorate it by cultivating and establishing the ground rules and backup plans in advance.

Most of the "how to" and advice books about selling companies were written by investment bankers. The implied denial and silence on the divided loyalties of investment bankers is a serious issue affecting every seller.

The companies belong to the sellers until a sale is completed and the money changes hands, making the buyer the new owner. That's an obvious but important point that sellers need to keep in mind. In most cases, the company in play is the largest single asset of the sellers. While the selling process is underway, it's critical that business owners are extraordinarily protective of their precious asset. Many companies have been damaged and even destroyed during the selling process.

It's not over till it's over! If something goes wrong during negotiations or with the business, the sellers need to remain in control of all their options. This may include a range of possibilities, including aborting the process altogether, taking a "time-out" to fix the problem, or pursuing a different strategy altogether, such as selling some assets of the company but not the entire company, selling out to key employees with private equity partners, or establishing an ESOP (Employee Stock Ownership Plan).

Prudent stewardship dictates that owners have contingency plans, exit routes, and safety nets as the sales process unfolds. The seller has the most at stake and the greatest risk during this fragile process. Therefore, the seller must keep control and be ready to pull the trigger on alternatives when the situation dictates a change in direction is necessary.

It's important to have contingency plans prepared in advance and remain in a state of readiness to execute them. Spend time in the beginning developing plans—there are tremendous benefits to having them—it's your insurance policy against a botched effort. The investment bankers virtually never discuss this possibility—not because they never experienced it. But when things go wrong, bankers want to control the situation—most often convincing the seller to conclude the deal at a lower price! After all, when a deal begins to crater, the investment banker is faced with losing all of their investment in getting the sale to the point of "almost" closing. They are eager to figure out how to get the deal done even if it's less advantageous to the seller.

If you've been a player in the industry or the market segment in which you operate, you know the other players better than your advisors do; and you are better positioned to react to significant problems that might affect the underlying value of the company. Having a solid backup plan also gives you more strength in dealing with buyers and causes them to feel the urgency to complete the deal on your terms if, in fact, they really want to make the acquisition.

There must be competition for the buyer, even if there isn't. Simply having an investment banker represent the seller makes a strong statement. It indicates seriousness about selling and sends a message to prospective buyers that you're not willing to be charmed into selling to a single prospective buyer. The professionalism and objectivity an investment banker brings to the process implies underlying competitiveness among the buyers.

A professionally prepared offering memorandum (a black book) speaks volumes to prospective buyers. It says, this company is going to be sold and the seller and the selling team are in control of this process, *at least at the outset.*

It's only when a buyer thinks they're the only party in the negotiation—or the only serious prospective buyer and the seller's only opportunity to sell—that they begin to take advantage of their power position. The only way to neutralize this tactic is to always have alternatives right up to the point of the wire transfer.

Delaying and requesting more and more information from the seller is a tactic used by many buyers to make the sellers off balance and worried. It's important for the seller to know as much as possible about the buyer's reasons for making the acquisition.

This knowledge alone gives the buyer more power to enforce the deadlines for getting the deal done and recognize enforcement is far easier when the buyer is threatened by the existence of viable backup options.

There are two types of sales for family companies. The first is an inside sale to family members and employees. The second is a sale to outsiders. There are options in each type.

Inside Sales

1. Dividend Strip of Owners: This is something I did a few years before selling the company to provide liquidity to the shareholders. We got a professional appraisal to establish the market value of the company and prepared a prospectus for the banks in order to borrow the money. Our plan was to take 50 percent of the appraised value out of the company in a super dividend. The total amounted to two and half times book value and was supported by the cash flow of the company. Three of the major banks in Milwaukee agreed to provide the funds in a term note with no personal guarantees. The New York investment bankers didn't think it could be done with smaller banks in the Midwest.

2. Sale to Family Members: The same kind of financing as in a dividend strip can be set up to finance the sale of stock to siblings or the next generation.

3. Sale to Employees: There are many tax-advantaged methods for selling ownership of the company to the employees. Tax advisors and attorneys are able to provide all of the information about these alternatives.

Inside sales provide the easiest option for monetizing the shares of the owners with the need or desire to do so. While not the best alternative for maximizing shareholder value, it is a formulaic approach that can be done efficiently and quietly.

Outside Sales

1. Private Equity Firm/Financial Buyer: These buyers have more tolerance for risk and debt than family business owners. They are principally interested in taking cost out of the companies they purchase, pay down their debt, and sell the company in five to seven years. It's strictly a financial deal with little concern for a company's culture or the employees. Making related acquisitions for minimal equity and maximum debt is also a part of the strategy for building value quickly.

2. Strategic Buyer: These buyers have clear strategic reasons for purchasing a company, which may allow them to pay more money for an acquisition than alternative buyers with no strategic reasons. A typical example is purchase by a competitor who is, in effect, consolidating the industry. There are tremendous opportunities to merge competitors and substantially reduce duplicated and redundant costs. Strategic buyers can have a myriad of reasons to acquire another company such as product line extension, entry into new markets and gaining new customers, expanding the geographic footprint, and creating management opportunities for staff members.

3. Public Offering: Few companies are candidates for an IPO. There are many criteria and requirements to be met before a

company can begin the process of going public. Your accountants and lawyers will be helpful in guiding you through the process. It's also a good idea to talk to others who have already done it. The two main advantages for a family company to go public, if you meet the requirements, are to provide shareholders a system to sell shares and achieve liquidity and to be able to raise needed capital for expansion through the public equity markets.

Important Requirements

Before considering any kind of sale or recapitalization, it is imperative to have audited financial statements from a reputable and respected CPA firm, preferably in either the Big Four or the second tier of firms. It is also wise to have a confidential, professional valuation prepared for your company. Finally, you should be aware of the debt capacity of your company learned by interviewing lenders.

Selling a family business is typically a once-in-a-lifetime event and should be done with extreme care and precision.

It is easy to botch the sale of a company, and the result of doing so can be catastrophic. Investment bankers (business brokers) can make fatal mistakes by not being acquainted with the optimum buyers in your market. They can present your company poorly and miss the hidden selling points.

The timing of going to market is critical. Performance of the company should be strong, facilitating a powerful story to prospective buyers. Problems should be cleaned up prior to embarking on a selling effort. Conditions in the market should provide a positive climate for selling the company.

Buyers have extensive experience in making acquisitions, while sellers have only one company to sell. Therefore, the playing field is not level. To have a successful sale requires that the seller is replete with talented and experienced people on the selling team. This is the only way to equalize the expertise.

Successfully selling a family business is an art and requires a disciplined process. There are four distinct periods:

1. Exploration
2. Decision Making
3. Execution
4. Postsale

The previous chapter presented Exploration and Decision Making. This chapter presents the process for the Execution period, and the next discusses the Postsale period.

Execution Period

Once the final decision is made, the selling team and key owners will take the process forward. *To maintain confidentiality,* information flow and exchange should be limited, including to family members. Everyone with knowledge that the process is commencing should be sworn to secrecy. If word gets out that the company is being sold, competitors will flock to customers and employees will be vulnerable to alternative employment offers. It can cause reduction in the value of the company.

The company should be cleaned up—problems resolved or eliminated—and ready to sell. The "black book" offering memorandum and selling materials should be professionally prepared with integrity. Taking shortcuts and making misrepresentations can radically undermine a successful process.

Selling to an informed buyer is also important. A prospective buyer's understanding and appreciation of the business will go a long way toward keeping the process on track. That's not to say there are ill-informed buyers out there with more money than sense, but planning a selling strategy to shake down a sucker isn't good business. A business that has been built with caring passion by the owner-managers and has the potential to continue prospering and providing jobs for the employees should be put in the hands of the best, most responsible buyer.

Problems—most notably in the due diligence phase—can be significantly minimized by having reliable, audited financial statements and well-documented financial records. A highly respected CPA firm presenting the financial reports of the company can add tremendous credibility and make prospective buyers more comfortable.

Virtually all due diligence can be limited to the accounting firm's offices if the financial statements are audited and presented by a reputable certified public accountant, preferably a large regional, national, or international firm with an impeccable reputation.

Whatever additional information the prospective buyer needs is generally found in the work papers at the accounting firm, or the information can be funneled through them to the buyer.

It's impossible to maintain any semblance of confidentiality if there are representatives of the buyer rooting around looking for information in the seller's offices. It is also disruptive to the ongoing operation of the business.

To achieve the best outcome, a disciplined process is required. It is broken down in four segments as follows:

1. Creating the Selling Team
2. Positioning the Company
3. Finding the Buyer
4. Closing the Sale

Creating the Selling Team

The first step in the execution period involves forming the selling team. Like any other important assignment, the choice of talent to employ and the composition of the team will make a big difference in the outcome. Even if your company is small, it is critical to put together a group of individuals who are experienced in mergers, acquisitions, and sale transactions. The intricacies of executing a deal are numerous and complex. The process is unforgiving, and no tolerance for substandard work exists. In selecting and appointing the selling team, family business owners need to exercise great care.

- *Selection of advisors*
  Ordinarily, influencers play an important role in recommending advisors or reinforcing their selection for the selling transaction.

The advisors are the lawyers and accountants who will be involved in the process. They may or may not be the company's regular lawyers and accountants. Many sellers have learned the hard way that there is a tremendous imbalance of experience between buyers and sellers of companies. Therefore, knowledgeable sellers will use only professional advisors—lawyers and accountants—who have actively and successfully handled multiple sale transactions. Only this way can sellers narrow the experience gap and equalize the buying and selling processes.

Advisors play a pivotal role in handling the legal, financial, and tax matters that are part of consummating a successful transaction. For the sellers, mistakes and poor advice can have grave, long-standing, and expensive consequences. Family business owners should therefore take extreme care in searching for, screening, selecting, and appointing their professional advisors.

- *Evaluation and selection of intermediaries*
Intermediaries are the investment bankers and business brokers. The best ones are those who have consummated the most successful transactions on behalf of *similar* companies. They should have solid reputations with both buyers and sellers and *excellent references* and be well regarded among the most logical buyers for the selling company. References should always be thoroughly checked among sellers and buyers who have worked with the firm. Mutual respect and good chemistry *must* characterize the relationship between the selected investment bankers and the sellers they represent.

During the evaluation phase, the family business owners should consider no questions they want to ask as impertinent or out of bounds. Once the selling process has begun, changing investment bankers is very difficult, if not impossible. Because first impressions can be deceiving and the stakes are too high to risk a mistake, thorough research is imperative.

Getting a solid prediction of the expected market value is essential. Checking references to figure out the gaps between the investment banker's projections and the actual yields is an effective screening mechanism for family business leaders.

Reviewing the investment banker's tombstones and the particulars of completed transactions is a good starting point. Prospect lists of potential acquirers provide family business leaders with further insight. They help to authenticate the investment banker's market knowledge and creativity in identifying buyer prospects. And be sure to verify the number of transactions they've actually done with the potential buyers they've identified to determine the depth of their relationships in your industry segment. The greater the number of viable and interested prospective acquirers, the more intense competitive bidding will be created for the selling company along with a higher purchase price in the end. Family business leaders identified the time spent evaluating investment bankers as extraordinarily beneficial. Many regret that they hadn't spent more time on it.

- *Selection of company team*

Family business leaders cite the selection of the company selling team as a critical task. Two major concerns during the selling process are maintaining confidentiality and minimizing disruption in the operation of the business. Therefore, limit the "inner circle" only to those employees with an absolute "need to know." The discretion of key company people who are working on the impending transaction is essential.

Key people who are articulate and broadly knowledgeable about the company make the most effective team members. These individuals represent the quality of people prospective buyers will expect to find in the company. The team should also represent the management continuity the buyer may be looking to acquire.

Positioning the Company

The manner in which selling companies are positioned in the minds of prospective acquirers can have a profound effect on pricing. The prospects for future growth and development, beyond past performance, are "imbedded" in positioning. Family business leaders can present companies for exactly what they have been and for what they are now. Or they can present them for what they can become. While family business leaders, investment bankers, and professional advisors have all explained that buyers will not pay "full price" for "blue sky," they will pay a premium for companies with excellent growth prospects, if demanded by the sellers. It is therefore financially responsible for sellers to devote time to examining how their companies can be positioned to generate the best possible price.

- **_Developing the selling strategy_**
  Developing a cogent selling strategy can make a big difference in the outcome of the sale. Determining in advance precisely how the seller's company will fit with prospective buyers' companies has proven effective. Being able to demonstrate how buyers can increase revenues and reduce costs by acquiring the seller's company is an important positioning strategy. Greater benefit will accrue to sellers who can show that synergistic gains are likely to follow the merger of the acquiring and acquired companies. Identifying the success of past initiatives and applying them to future plans can be effective in painting a picture of the exceptional opportunities available to the buyer.
- **_Preparing the company for sale_**
  Family business leaders should prepare their companies for sale. They should identify (if not initiate) any "tough-minded" moves the buyer might make to clean up inefficiencies and capitalize on new opportunities. Sellers should try to position themselves so they can reap the rewards for immediate improvements the buyer may make on ideas with which the seller is knowledgeable.

  Sellers should also discontinue or restructure losing operations for future success. Owner benefits (perks) should be clearly identified so their cost can be added back to the restated earnings presented to the prospective buyers.
- **_Preparation of "the book"_**
  Preparation of the selling documents— "the book"—is the responsibility of the investment banker. Successful sellers have reported better results when they let the investment banker develop the initial "draft" in order to get any fresh, innovative

thinking from the investment banker *and then* make the revisions they think appropriate. While sellers should expect disagreements about the selling approach, they should not merely yield to the wishes of the investment bankers because they have more experience selling companies. Strategic understanding, market knowledge, and operating experience are exceedingly valuable when preparing the selling documents. Sellers should never abdicate involvement, because they may have a much deeper understanding of the fundamental value and the intricacies of their companies. However, they should remain open to new angles from the investment banker.

Books (selling memoranda) should be tailored and targeted to specific types of buyers—financial or strategic. There are many variations among strategic buyers and the way they see integrating the acquisition into their operations. If the content of the book precisely matches the value proposition of each individual potential buyer, the chance of getting a higher price increases.

- *Selection of prospective purchasers*

Investment bankers should be knowledgeable about the active buyers in the market segments they serve. They should be aware of all the strategic buyers as well as all of the financial buyers, and they should be able to provide a complete and interesting prospect list, including demonstrating knowledge of the decision-making individuals at the prospect companies. After careful review of the list provided by the investment banker, the seller should supplement the list. This process should actually happen while the sellers are evaluating the investment bankers. This is an appropriate test of the investment banker's market knowledge.

The seller should carefully screen and *approve* the list so that solicitations of interest are never targeted at prospective buyers with whom the seller would be uncomfortable sharing confidential information. The seller should also prioritize prospective purchasers and develop a unique selling strategy for each.

Finding the Buyer

The investment banker will run the selling process with the approval of the seller. At all times the seller should carefully monitor all of the investment banker's selling activities and nurture close communications throughout the process.

- *Solicitation of interest*

    Thorough discussions should take place prior to contacting any prospective buyers, and the seller should clearly understand exactly how the investment banker is conducting the solicitations of interest. This understanding is important and needs to be factored into responding to unanticipated and unwanted leaks during the process. The sellers should definitely be in control of the investment banker's solicitation process. The investment banker should not contact any prospective buyer without the seller's permission, and the seller should know not only what the banker is saying but also the timing of the calls.

    To solicit interest, the investment banker or intermediary calls the prospective buyer and shares basic information of the company being offered for sale. If the prospect is interested, the banker will lay out a timetable for the selling process, including time frames for reviewing the book and the deadline for receiving letters of intent. The due diligence period and process is described, and the expected closing date is established.

- *Confidentiality agreements*

    When potential buyers express interest, it is essential to execute *confidentiality agreements* (often called NDAs—nondisclosure agreements) that cover the content of discussions and all materials shared with prospective buyers. Experienced acquirers understand the seller's sensitivity and desire for complete confidentiality, but unsophisticated and inexperienced buyers lack that appreciation. Therefore, the investment banker's explanations of the importance of confidentiality must be crystal clear. In spite of all best efforts, there will be leaks, so a plan needs to be in place for responding to rumors with plausible explanations and for damage control.

An acceptable response might be: "We are 'in play' in the market—first as a buyer to participate in industry consolidation; second as a strategic partner or merger candidate; and perhaps as a seller if it turns out to be the best strategic alternative." But now we don't know what the end point may be. We want to make sure we are properly positioned in a changing market. When we know something definite, we'll let you know."

- **Distribution of "the books"**
  Following the execution of confidentiality agreements, copies of "the book" are sent to potential buyers. The "book" should contain all of the information required for a buyer to be able to make an informed evaluation of the company and reach a decision about making an offer based on the information that has been made available.

- **Letters of intent**
  Well-run, disciplined sales processes conducted by professional investment bankers have established timetables. Reasonable time frames are set up for the prospective buyers to review the book and make a decision of whether to proceed. If the prospective buyer is uninterested, they are required to return the book by the deadline. If the prospective buyer is interested in acquiring the selling company, a nonbinding letter of intent (LOI) is submitted to the investment banker within the deadline period (the letter includes the basic terms and conditions of an offer, subject to due diligence).

- **Selection of the purchaser**
  Sellers typically select the buyer from the group of potential acquirers who have submitted letters of intent. If the sellers are unhappy with the companies that have made offers, or the offers are inadequate, they may widen the field of prospects or decide to reverse the decision to sell and make a recommitment to company ownership.

  If there is an appropriate prospective buyer who has submitted an acceptable letter of intent, a process and timetable are agreed upon to "go to contract," reach a final agreement, and conduct due diligence.

Buyers are generally selected according to the following criteria: terms and conditions of the financial offer, reputation of the purchaser, and cultural fit with the seller under the circumstances.

Closing the Sale

Closing the sale is a vexing process. Letters of intent are nonbinding, and winning bidders often exploit the opportunity to get into companies and embark on the due diligence process (a hunting expedition) with the objective of making discoveries that will reduce the previously agreed upon purchase price.

Another complicating factor mentioned earlier is the tendency of investment bankers to gradually shift their efforts toward providing greater support for the buyers' positions, rather than the sellers'. Investment banking fees are tied to the success of the transaction. If there is no transaction, the fee is tiny or none at all. Therefore, in the concluding stages of a sale, the investment bankers seem to work hardest to cajole the seller into making compromises that will facilitate a transaction. Exceptions to this behavior among investment bankers exist, but they are atypical. There are several explanations for this dynamic.

First, there will be no transaction if the seller will not agree to the final terms of the buyer's offer. Discoveries made by the buyer during due diligence would undoubtedly be the same for a succession of buyers, so if the seller is willing to sell, it is far easier and less costly to consummate a deal rather than repeating the process with another prospective buyer.

Second, the seller of a family company has but one transaction to make, whereas a buyer is typically in the market to make multiple transactions. The seller is, therefore, a "one-shot" customer for the investment banker. The buyer, however, represents an annuity and can provide multiple transactions on both the buy and sell sides.

- *Offer to purchase*
  When the buyer replaces the letter of intent with a bona fide agreement or contract, the terms and conditions may be different

from what the seller envisioned. Negotiations ensue in order to close or resolve any gaps. Once the buyer and seller reach agreement on the terms of the contract, due diligence begins.

- *Due diligence*

Naturally, buyers do not want to pay for anything they are not getting. Nor do they want to pay full price for something they subsequently discover has diminished value. So, buyers intently search for such variances. Due diligence teams from buyer companies are rewarded for finding "weaknesses" on which they can negotiate price reductions. They are also fearful of missing factors that can turn into big problems after the deal closes, so they tend to scrutinize everything.

For the seller, due diligence is the most difficult part of the closing process. By the time due diligence begins, the seller is nearly worn out by the intensity of the process to date. Sellers yearn for closing, and what they feel will be the ultimate relief of stress. They are ready to have the entire transaction behind them, only to be faced with what can be the most debilitating phase of the selling process. The prospective buyer knows nearly everything about the seller's company—and therefore, because of the knowledge the buyer has about the seller's company, the power shifts from seller to buyer. Walking away from a transaction is also much easier for a buyer than a seller. There are far more negatives for the seller when a deal goes sour. Embarrassing information can be revealed, and it can be difficult to get the company back on track, whereas the buyer in an aborted deal just continues business as usual.

Sellers can and should have a safety net in place for just this kind of problem. It may be the establishment of an ESOP (Employee Stock Ownership Plan) or a sale to the management team with a venture capital firm or a private equity investor. All of these alternatives should be examined as part of the selling process, and if it's ever necessary, reverting to a backup plan can relieve a tremendous amount of pressure. The price may be lower, but there may be other psychic and even financial benefits that can offset the shortfall. The mere appearance of an acceptable backup plan can neutralize a buyer's power position in the final stages of the selling process and help to keep the sale on track in a fair and equitable manner.

When a sale process is terminated during the execution period, it is usually because of a serious problem discovered during due diligence. Generally, it is a case of the terms being materially changed or the buyer walking away for some reason. It is understandably a severe blow to the sellers, and a passionate recommitment to company ownership can be very difficult. When a sale falls apart late in the game, the best option for sellers is to set about fixing any problems and work hard to get ready for the next trigger point or opportunity to sell.

- *Consummating the sale*

  The first moments after consummating a sale have been described as a "surreal" feeling. No one who sold a company for the first time had any idea what to expect, but most people who have experienced a sale describe it as rather "anticlimactic." Agonizing over the decision and going through an arduous selling process create a sense of expectation that the final event will be something special. Rather, it generally ends with an innocuous wire transfer and a confirmation of receipt of the funds by the bank. Closings usually take place in a lawyer's conference room in another city, and the transfer of funds follows the completion of signing dozens of official documents. While it is the culmination of months of intense activity, the actual closing can be something of a letdown—like a blip on an oscilloscope.

The decision-making process can be slow, laborious, and excruciatingly difficult, and once the decision to sell is reached, sellers often think the execution process is mechanical, efficient, and can be done in good time. Wrong!

The selling process, as explained by investment bankers, appears straightforward, and while they might indicate it can be done in six to nine months, nine months to a year or longer is more accurate if done right. This is assuming that the seller is basically starting at the beginning of the execution process.

Due diligence by the buyer can be the most debilitating part of the process. The buyer is focused on finding problems—problems that will open the door to renegotiation and lowering the agreed upon price or, in the worst case, killing the deal.

Finally, if the timetable for closing is in the buyer's control, the seller is helpless in attempting to keep the process on schedule. In my own case, I realized the buyer was employing stalling tactics. However, when I informed our investment banker that I had an equally attractive alternative and gave notice that I was going to announce the outcome four weeks later on a date certain, the buyer eagerly came back with a sense of urgency. The stalling ended, and we closed on the final deadline I presented.

When the buyers perceive their offer as the only viable alternative, they will take advantage of their power position. That's why it's important to have a contingency plan (a backup buyer) until the deal is closed and the funds have been received in the seller's account.

One final thought:

Buyers often say they want the seller to stay after the sale is completed, but they really don't, unless they feel a need to help keep customers, suppliers, and employees during the transition period. It's natural that buyers are going to want to change things, and keeping the former owner/manager in place will be a big impediment to their progress.

Changes in the business made by the new owners can be insulting to the sellers—who question what the new owners are doing to ruin or even kill their baby. Conflict always ensues and it's miserable. Why some sellers submit themselves to this brain damage—even temporarily—I'll never understand.

Key executives are different—they've had bosses and worked for owners throughout their careers. Their lived experience is much different from owners'. They may like working for the seller; however, they will be able to make a transition to a new boss and owner or find another job—far easier than it will be for the former owner to adapt to an environment where someone else is calling the shots and naming the tunes.

It's just best for the sellers to move on and graciously offer to be available for any consultation the new owners may need or want. When Art Nielsen sold the A. C. Nielsen Company to Dunn & Bradstreet, he told me they appointed him their sex consultant after the sale. I curiously asked what that meant. He said, "When they want my *f…g* advice, they'll ask for it." He never heard from them again after the sale.

Postsale Period

The postsale period begins at the point the seller confirms the receipt of the proceeds and the buyer takes possession of the just purchased company. The aftershocks will be discussed in the next chapter.

CHAPTER 5

AFTERSHOCKS: LIFE AFTER THE SALE

S elling a family-owned company can be traumatic; therefore, careful thought should be given to anticipating the feelings of all the stakeholders after the sale is completed and the family no longer owns it. Otherwise, it's a very difficult period for all the people involved to go through.

- In concert with the buyer, a comprehensive communications plan should be developed to ensure a smooth transition from the sellers to the buyers and to overcome the fears of the people associated with the company
- Develop a postsale vision for the business family
- Revisit the family's mission and values
- Update the family constitution (if there is one)
- Create guidelines, policies, and rules for the management of family wealth
- Create a new agenda for the family council to sustain the legacy of the business family

A significant postsale danger will emerge. Managing liquidity often creates vulnerabilities to opportunistic investment promoters—exposure to "deals" that look "too good to pass up"—to being lured into investments in which they have no knowledge or experience. Here are a few tips:

1. Be patient.
2. Be prudent (get good advice from people who have nothing to gain).
3. Remember, the original wealth was created with specialized knowledge, ingenuity, hard work, luck, and limited capital over a long period of time.
4. The objective is responsible stewardship.

The postsale period begins immediately after the wire transfer and the buyer takes possession of the just purchased company. It is a time of great change and adjustment for everyone associated with the company. This chapter presents the postsale aftershocks the family business leaders, family members, employees, stakeholders, and community members typically experience.

Too many successful business owners think they can strike gold again and again. Some can, but more can't and make mistakes with their newly gotten liquid wealth. It's best to be conservative and preserve the financial resources required for security. Having a pool of funds with which to gamble is fine, particularly if there's enough that a loss won't hurt. Otherwise it's far better to share wisdom and advice and take a carried interest (one you don't have to pay for) in new ventures following the same bootstrapping entrepreneurial philosophy found in the heritage of the company just sold.

Sellers should take a break and relax. Take time to reflect and engage in some stimulating educational and philanthropic activities. A mentoring/advisory role for someone else can be a satisfying and worthwhile activity during the period following a sale. Don't make a big commitment—either with time or money—until the dust has really settled and a considered decision can be made.

The idea of being a passive investor is often oversimplified. It's typically not in the DNA of successful owner/managers. More often than not, the junior partner in a new activity you are backing won't work out, and you'll be forced to saddle up again and assume a tight grip on the reins of the new enterprise, if that possibility exists in your investment agreement. Be careful and cautious.

Get the best possible advice available on managing a safe nest egg that will provide a lifetime of financial security. Selecting financial managers is serious business. Do it carefully. Set conservative financial benchmarks and monitor performance. Keep in mind that the cost of switching to a new advisor if you're not happy can be enormous when a new money manager reconfigures your portfolio.

Thoughts about philanthropy are important at this juncture.

Charitable remainder trusts can accomplish several objectives:

- Provide lifetime income to the grantors
- Provide a large tax deduction at the time they are established
- Fulfill a charitable goal to a favorite institution

A business owner on whose board I was a member chose to direct his own investments following the sale of his company. Initially he discovered and invested in tech stocks and looked extraordinarily successful—until the dot-com bust. Then he decided to switch his remaining portfolio out of tech stocks into something he felt he understood more. Selling his holdings resulted in significant tax consequences—losing even more of his portfolio. Then he invested a substantial portion of what he had left in a private equity deal underwriting a business that had developed a process for pasteurizing eggs. Having been in the food business, he thought he understood this investment opportunity and would have the chance for greater involvement, but not control.

Unfortunately, through a series of miscalculations and management mistakes, the egg-pasteurizing business didn't make it, and he lost his total investment and ended up with a small fraction of his business sale proceeds. What remained provided a far more modest income than he and his wife had planned to support them in their later years. The stress he experienced as an investor and director of the egg business contributed to his stroke, severely declining health and his ultimate death. I had a front-row seat for this show, as I also made an investment in this ill-fated venture recommended by my former colleague but fortunately not to the degree he and his brother had. I learned an important lesson.

When business owners who have had a major illiquid asset suddenly have seemingly enormous liquid wealth, they can become less careful and more trusting than they were with their own company. That's why it's important to have the very best (conservative) financial advisors available and maintain the same diligence and discipline that facilitated the creation of wealth in the first place. At this stage, I think it's more important to preserve what we have rather than take excessive risk to make more. If risk is our choice, we're better off taking it with the business we truly know and understand.

It's far easier to lose a fortune than it is to make one.
—*The Gospel of Wealth*, by Andrew Carnegie

Selling has the biggest effect on family CEOs because their identities and lives change the most. Their focal point is suddenly gone. Family business leaders don't anticipate their postsale emotions when they are working intently on the sale of their companies. Leaders who opt to remain with acquiring companies can be optimistic about challenges and opportunities ahead.

Sellers have felt that they had not only achieved financial independence but would also now have the opportunity to further build their former companies through acquisitions using the resources of the deep-pocketed buyers and not feel any pressure from family member shareholders about the possibility of making mistakes and dissipating family wealth.

These promises soon turn into disappointment. Executives at acquiring companies can be disdainful or resentful of the former business owners who hit the jackpot, and they are no longer inclined to treat them with the respect previously afforded them during the courtship period. The new owners are immediately focused on integrating their new acquisition into their culture. Having the former CEO around is not helpful, and therefore, the former CEO is immediately marginalized.

There is also a large impact on the shareholders of the family company, other family members, nonfamily employees, and other stakeholders. A range of feelings prevails, including a sense of excitement and anticipation; uncertainty and fear; and guilt and betrayal.

Effect on Family Business Leaders
A pattern emerged through interviews with family business leaders after the sale. Emotions are not dissimilar to stages in Elizabeth Kubler Ross's

seminal book, *On Death and Dying*. The feelings described by leaders of companies that have been sold accurately fit in the following categories:

1. Euphoria
2. Disconnectedness
3. Depression
4. Realism
5. Optimism
6. Action

Following are quotes from sellers that illuminate each of the stages.

Euphoria

A feeling of intense happiness, self-confidence, or well-being sometimes exaggerated in pathological states as mania

It was a surreal feeling for me after I talked to my banker and learned the wire for the full purchase price had arrived at the bank and was deposited in my account. Within six minutes, I scratched of my name off my business card and carefully printed the name of the new chairman. I had capitalized my life's work and felt a tremendous sense of relief and happiness. And then I wondered if the plane would have an adequate supply of Canadian Club for my flight home.

In the first days and weeks following the sale of their family companies, other family CEOs indicated that they experienced a sense of unbounded euphoria. They had accomplished their objectives and successfully sold their family companies. They had achieved financial security and were free of the constant worry and stress associated with the ownership and leadership of their enterprises. They felt relief, satisfaction, pride, and happiness.

The recollections of family business leaders after selling and leaving their companies capture their euphoria.

*I started this business with very little capital and what
turned out to be a good idea. I was fortunate to be able to
hire good people who worked hard and built the company.
After nearly thirty years we were able to make a great
sale and become the platform in the United States for
a highly respected international company. Our entire
management team continued to lead the US business for
the new owners. For the first time, my wife and I had all
the liquidity we needed and the time to really enjoy it.*
—FOUNDER

*We had always had personal debt. Immediately after
the sale, I paid off all of my debt, and it felt wonderful.
I was completely debt-free and my new challenge
would be to become a wise investor. I was really
happy and excited. I almost couldn't believe it.*
—COUSIN CEO

*It was a wonderful feeling to know that I had created
financial security through trusts for four generations and
my wife and I were able to do things we had always thought
about, but now we didn't have financial constraints.*
—CONTROLLING OWNER

*The idea of being able to have the opportunity to
pursue a variety of entrepreneurial ventures and
mentor young people was exhilarating.*
—FOUNDER

*For the first time, I realized that I would be able to travel
just for fun, and have quality time to spend with my wife
and family. I could finally have the freedom and flexibility
to do exactly what I wanted to do when I wanted to do it.*
—COUSIN CEO

Family business leaders describe the period immediately following the sale of their family companies as a time when they felt "happy" and "satisfied" about having made a significant accomplishment.

Disconnectedness

Breakdown of communication, disjointed, broken, severed, withdrawn

In the days following the sale of our company, my phone was ringing off the hook. Friends and well-wishers were calling to congratulate me and wish me a happy retirement. They were curious about what I was going to do now after the sale and how I was going to spend my time. Then, after about two weeks, my phone stopped ringing. It was like it had been disconnected. The only calls I was receiving were from investment counsellors who wanted to manage my new liquidity. As time went on, it was clear that I was out of the game. I became anxious and realized my power base had been stripped away. I was feeling like I had nothing substantive to do. I knew I was just moping around with no purpose.

After selling, other family business leaders described going through a rather quiet, but anxiety-filled period. They too reported that their phones stopped ringing. They began to feel cut off from many of the people with whom they had had regular contact. While they anticipated not having relationships with their former companies, the reality differed radically from what they expected. They felt empty. Several felt completely disconnected and wondered if they would be able to fill the huge void that had become so apparent.

> *After resting and feeling that I had gotten my*
> *personal things organized, I began to feel like I was*
> *at loose ends. And I was getting the sense that I was*
> *irritating my wife and interrupting her life.*
> —*FOUNDER*

*I was having difficulty developing a routine. I didn't
have a place to go every day. It really seemed strange.*
—Sɪʙʟɪɴɢ CEO

*I didn't think I would, but I missed the
camaraderie with my colleagues.*
—Cᴏɴᴛʀᴏʟʟɪɴɢ Oᴡɴᴇʀ

*I thought I wanted to be finished solving
problems, being in a leadership role and having
people depend on me. After being away from
it for a while, I started longing for it.*
—Cᴏɴᴛʀᴏʟʟɪɴɢ Oᴡɴᴇʀ

*I didn't feel as though I had anything important to do
anymore. I was embarrassed telling friends that I was retired.*
—Cᴏɴᴛʀᴏʟʟɪɴɢ Oᴡɴᴇʀ

*When you're out of the game, people look at you
differently. I could feel it, and I didn't like it.*
—Sɪʙʟɪɴɢ CEO

*My support system was gone—my secretary, chief financial
officer and others I had relied on to help me with anything
I needed to do. I felt lost. I hadn't realized how dependent
I had become. I felt like I had far too much busy work and
no support to get it done. It was frustrating and lonely.*
—Cᴏɴᴛʀᴏʟʟɪɴɢ Oᴡɴᴇʀ

*Managing a portfolio held none of the excitement
for me that managing a company did.*
—Sɪʙʟɪɴɢ CEO

*I hadn't imagined how much I would miss
my industry friends and events.*
—Cᴏᴜsɪɴ CEO

*I began to feel useless. The company was functioning
without me and on those infrequent occasions when someone
from the company would call me to discuss an issue, I
knew I was powerless and could do nothing about it.*
—Controlling Owner

Many others conveyed similar feelings through anecdotes about the period following the sales of their companies.

Depression

Sadness, gloom; dejection, dullness, inactivity

Months after I had sold, I felt like I was becoming depressed. I was eating too much, drinking too much, and not exercising regularly. In spite of the fact that I had hooked up with a local executive who was looking for a company to buy that he could run, and he invited me to join him in his search, it gave me no juice. He wanted me to be the nonexecutive chairman and an investor. It didn't hold much interest for me at all. I didn't know what I wanted at that point in my life. I was missing people at my company and wondering what was going on there. I was developing tremendous anxiety and having trouble sleeping. In addition, I learned that my closest colleague at the company, who retired a month after I did, had terminal cancer. He died six months later. I was devastated.

Other family business leaders who sold their companies described periods of loneliness following the sale. They reported feelings of loss of relevance, and some talked about feeling lethargic and enervated. Some realized at the time that they were sinking into depression, which was particularly difficult since they had perceived their decision to sell as being well considered. They thought they were better prepared for life after leading their family companies than they actually were. While they tried to focus on the fact that they had accomplished their goals and had achieved financial security, they missed the action and just plain felt empty. This period is best described as "sad" and "difficult."

Being around so much was difficult for my wife. It was obvious that I was getting on her nerves and that was upsetting to me.
—*FOUNDER*

For the first time in my life, I felt very lonely.
—*SIBLING CEO*

I felt like I had lost motivation to do anything. I was lethargic and found myself taking naps every day.
—*CONTROLLING OWNER*

With all the time I had available, I figured I would finally be able to get in shape. The opposite happened. I was eating too much, drinking too much and not exercising. I was caught in a downward spiral, and I didn't know how to get out of it.
—*CONTROLLING OWNER*

I felt anxious, I'm not sure why, but that's how I was feeling a good deal of the time. I was also irritable. It seems that little, trivial things bothered me more than they ever had before.
—*CONTROLLING OWNER*

I had always had goals-I didn't have any anymore.
—*CONTROLLING OWNER*

Some of the family business leaders frankly described the feelings they were experiencing as "depression," but all who had sold their companies and departed went through a period of similar symptoms.

Realism

Interest in or concern for the actual or real, as distinguished from the abstract, speculative; the tendency to view or represent things as they really are

I had been successful in a difficult business in a challenging industry. Our successful sale provided more money than our family could spend, and I had been respected in my industry and my community. I was awarded a distinguished alumni award from my university. I had everything I ever dreamed of having, and instead of taking advantage of opportunities, I felt like I was becoming a lazy slob. What was wrong with me? I needed to get off my butt.

The family business leaders in our study had been owners and operators of successful family companies.

They had been in difficult positions on previous occasions and had been able to navigate through troubles, effectively solve problems, overcome obstacles, and achieve success. In the postsale period, they had no choice but to accept the stark reality that they had, in fact, sold their family companies. All had monetized their life's work and were wealthy, and they recognized that their wealth provided nearly unlimited options. This "realistic" assessment of their position laid the groundwork for optimism.

> *It happened late one morning, and I was just sitting around not doing anything. I was feeling down, and a little sorry for myself. The idea came to me that I could do anything I wanted to do. I certainly had the money, and I also had the capability—so I had to get off my butt and do something.*
> *—CONTROLLING OWNER*

> *I said, what the hell is going on? I've had a very successful career. I'm financially secure and independent. I've created family wealth. And I feel like I'm sinking. I've got to do something about it.*
> *—SIBLING CEO*

> *I was in a bad state. I felt stuck, and I knew I needed to make a big change. I was always able to solve business problems, and I wondered why I was having trouble moving forward with my life. I thought about how much I had to offer, and how could I get into a position to share what I knew with others. I needed to talk to other people who might have been faced with the*

> *same situation, so I started calling people and getting together*
> *with them in an effort to pick up ideas that could help me.*
> —*FOUNDER*

As they assessed their situations more "realistically," family business leaders reached similar revelations and around that time decided to think optimistically about the next phase of their lives.

Optimism

> *A disposition or tendency to look on the more favorable side of events or*
> *conditions and to expect the most favorable outcome*

I had completed a program called the Age of Options at Harvard Business School months before the sale of my company was final. I had decided I wanted to teach and lecture part time and live in European capitals for a few months each year. What was I waiting for? I had done nothing to execute my plan. Perhaps I thought for some reason, it was out of reach. Instead it just dropped in my lap. I was invited to a graduate business school in Switzerland along with receiving invitations to lecture at other universities. I just needed to go after it. So I quit moping around and got busy.

Family business leaders consistently recalled their determination not to be unhappy with the new circumstances that had resulted from their successful achievements. In various ways, all began scanning the horizon for interesting and fulfilling alternatives. They thought about their experiences, skill sets, and interests and began imagining activities in which they could become involved.

> *I realized I needed to be involved in something of importance.*
> *I wasn't sure what. Would it be business education or some*
> *socially responsible organization? When I began looking, I*
> *was amazed at the number of alternatives and opportunities.*
> —*CONTROLLING OWNER*

I knew I had to talk to people to get ideas, so I began calling business friends and acquaintances. Even though they had stopped calling me after we sold the company, they were all willing to take my calls and meet with me. Many expressed envy about the situation I was in and expressed a desire to join me soon. Those visits eased my mind.

—CONTROLLING OWNER

When I began shopping for opportunities, it was amazing how many there were, particularly with my financial capacity and liquidity. I learned there were many potential investment opportunities, and the executives and directors of the nonprofit organizations were all over me after I began expressing interest in taking on more active leadership roles. I realized I would have to pick the opportunities carefully, or I could easily become over committed again.

—FOUNDER

Once the family business leaders took a more realistic view of their situations and began reaching out for opportunities the way they had done in their successful business careers, a wave of optimism washed away feelings of disconnectedness and depression.

Action

An act that one consciously wills and may be characterized by physical or mental activity.

I accepted the opportunity to become an executive-in-residence at IMD in Switzerland and ended up staying for four years and completing my doctorate studying the sale of family businesses. I took one of my Harley-Davidson motorcycles (remember I am from Milwaukee) with me and toured Europe while I was there. It turned out to be a glorious four years full of new experiences and adventures. And when I returned to the United States, I accepted a professorship at the University of Wisconsin–Madison School of Business.

Former family business leaders whose companies had been sold needed to create new structure and rhythm for their lives. Some became involved in new businesses and many in educational and philanthropic activities.

> *We decided to move. We felt the change would give us a fresh start, and we would share the adventure of making new friends and getting established. It didn't take long, and I was back "in business" as an investor and mentor. I also became involved in developing a golf course—something totally different from anything I had ever done.*
> —*FOUNDER*

> *I joined the boards of a couple of companies in my industry. They needed my advice, and I really felt like I was contributing. The people at the companies knew me from the industry and respected me. I was able to develop excellent rapport with them and accomplish some things with the people that senior management was unable to. One of the companies was subsequently sold, and I was able to help the family business leader through the selling process. I assumed an advisory role in a few of the companies in which I invested. And I also became chairman of the board of a hospital in my community. I'm now as busy as I want to be and feel good about my life.*
> —*SIBLING CEO*

> *I think I'm going through the postsale process pretty quickly. I've watched some good friends make mistakes because they moved too quickly after selling their family companies. I don't want to make the same mistakes, so I'm taking my time. My son, son-in-law and I have looked at a few businesses to buy. I really think we'll end up doing something together again. But my role will be different. This time it will be their deal, and I'll be an advisor. I am on a couple of boards which I enjoy very much, and I'm having fun playing more golf and spending time at our new home in Florida. For now, I have plenty to do.*
> —*COUSIN CEO*

One of the family business leaders, after selling his company, began writing for his community newspaper, published a few books, and endowed a centre at a leading university for the study of midsized companies.

Once the family business leaders took action, they did it in much the same manner and style that they had used to run their successful companies. They identified opportunities and seized the ones they felt were most attractive and worthwhile. And they passionately applied their experience and wisdom to their new endeavors.

The former family business leaders who are the happiest and most content feel they have found balance. They are engaged in purposeful activity—whether business or volunteer. They continue to seek educational opportunities. They take time out for recreation and leisure, and they covet the time they are able to spend with their families.

There's no question that everyone looks upon those who have sold their companies differently. The former owners no longer have the influence or the cachet they had when they owned companies. Families who have sold their companies need to be aware that the way they are viewed changes. They are often looked upon as "rich" but no longer "in the game." Their importance is diminished, and it looks like they are "retired" even if they aren't.

On a sad note, some of the family business leaders after selling their companies didn't know what they didn't know about investing. They were vulnerable to being courted and invested too much of their newfound liquidity in businesses that didn't perform as promised. This happened in more cases than I ever would have expected. So much of their knowledge and wisdom came from their experience in their industries and in their companies—places where they were comfortable. Therefore, they had "informed" intuition. When they were without it, lack of knowledge about companies and industries in which they were unfamiliar did not serve them well. A few of the former leaders continued to think they were the smartest people in the room and overestimated the amount of capital they had to risk when getting involved in businesses they didn't know and understand. They had become vulnerable to articulate people who operated in grey areas and could not deliver as represented. It was regrettable to see their egos and hubris have so much negative influence on the responsible stewardship of their wealth.

Effect on Family Members

After the sale, family members experience a number of effects. Family members, who were shareholders but not employees of the company and supported the decision to sell, are happy with the outcome and the financial flexibility they now have as a result of liquidating their shares. They are now free to invest in whatever they are passionate about.

There are examples of family members who have resentment toward the family-member CEO and family members who worked in the company who may have received a premium in the sale over other nonemployee shareholders. In some cases, founders who had passed along ownership to the next generation (children who had contributed nothing to building the company) took umbrage at the windfalls their children received from the sale. Unfortunately, this cast a pall over what should have been a celebratory and happy event.

The toughest challenges were lifestyle disruptions, particularly those caused by the family business leaders in their spouses' lives. Family business leaders who had rarely been present were suddenly around all the time with little to do. They wanted to make up for lost time and were not sensitive to the lives of others. They failed to recognize that they may have chosen to change their lives and focus, but that didn't mean that everyone else around them had chosen to change theirs. Repeated examples came up of "newly freed" family business leaders who became intrusive in their spouses' and children's happy and balanced lives.

Some family business leaders felt badly that their children—who were now grown—were not interested in spending as much time with them as the former leaders would have liked. However, there were also examples of grown children who were thrilled about the prospect of the family business leader now having the time to help and support them in the pursuit of their own individual and unique interests and passions.

Family members were generally pleased overall with the decision to sell in spite of problematic adjustments. While sentimental about the passage of their family companies to new owners, family members were happy with the financial outcome and the corresponding relief from the leadership and ownership responsibilities they had carried.

Family business leaders were all concerned about what the buyers would do to their companies. Therefore, they tried to select prospective buyers who would "sustain" the cultures they had created. They tried to do everything they could to create the illusion that the decision to sell would be good for the employees in terms of future opportunities and greater security with larger organizations.

Appreciation events are a good idea after companies are sold. Celebration of the liquidity event and discussions about developing a new family mission are important steps to take to keep the business family together.

Effect on Nonfamily employees

Employees of the sold companies didn't readily share the sellers' positive views. After all, they had chosen to work for family companies and the families. In addition, they are generally not rewarded with a portion of sale proceeds, although several family owners chose to make large and final contributions to their profit-sharing plans. Successful family companies typically have excellent employee relations, so it's understandable that employees were at first disappointed and worried about the change in ownership. Some felt betrayed and even double-crossed because the family business leaders had often talked about their unique qualities, family cultures, and long-term visions of their organizations.

When employees learned that their company was going to be sold or had been sold, they felt uncertain about their roles and their futures. An unanticipated change had come upon them, and they were unprepared. Many expected the worst—anticipating reduction of benefits, revisions of compensation programs, and changes in the work environment. In some cases, those changes occurred; in others, they didn't.

Naturally, employees were unsettled when new owners promptly cut benefits and eliminated profit-sharing programs and employee events. Those who had never worked for another company had a new appreciation for what they had but perhaps never fully appreciated.

Many employees wondered what had *really* driven the families to sell. Those who knew about their companies' success found the sales incomprehensible. One employee said, "The company was successful, the family was wealthy and they seemed to love the business. I will never ever understand why they sold. I don't think the reasons they gave us were the real reasons."

Significant change followed the sales in all cases. The companies had to be integrated into the cultures, operating procedures, and styles of the acquirers. In every case, the CEO changed on the day of or soon after the sale. In many instances, the nonfamily chief operating officer remained with the company. This presence created an easier transition to the new ownership and corporate structure, because the resident manager was familiar to the employees.

In our case, several of our publishers left within a year after the sale to join other companies or start their own businesses. We were a learning organization, and with a few exceptions, we only hired people who had market and industry experience rather than publishing experience. We preferred to teach our people our unique approach to the publishing business. One of the proudest metrics of my career is the number of people who became presidents of other publishing companies—several much larger than ours—or started their own successful companies from scratch. And it was interesting that they emulated many aspects of our corporate culture in the companies they established or led.

After buying our company, the CEO of the acquiring company seemed to be critical of nearly everything we had done whenever he had the chance. It didn't play well for the people who liked working for our company and appreciated the way it was run.

The performance of the sold companies is mixed. Some of the corporate entities no longer exist. They were consolidated into the acquiring corporations and virtually disappeared. Some of the formerly successful product lines have vanished through either market changes or mismanagement by the new owners, or both. However, a few of the companies have continued to grow and are now stronger than ever. In all but one case I studied, the companies have been sold a second time and even a third, or the companies that acquired them have been sold. These repetitive ownership changes after the original company leaves family hands are a predictable sign of the times. This is due to the increasing incidents of consolidation and the fundamental lack of loyalty investors have to the individual businesses in their portfolios.

Merger and acquisition activity continues at a feverish pace, and acquirers have voracious appetites. This strong force suggests that more and more companies will be in play as public and private investors focus on growth and value creation through acquisitions.

Effect on Stakeholders

Suppliers and vendors may be changed to those favored by the acquiring company or ones with whom they are already doing business. Typically, soon after the acquisition, supplier relationships will be reviewed and evaluated against alternatives.

Customers are likely to remain unless the new owners disrupt the relationships or terms and conditions under which they have been operating.

The directors and executives of nonprofit organizations worry when locally based companies are sold. The worst case is that funding stops when new owners take over. The former owners may continue to be philanthropic, but the ball game changes, and the criteria for and amount of support may change.

CHAPTER 6

JONATHAN'S RULES

- **Create the strongest, most talented, and experienced selling team you can assemble**

  You cannot compromise on this rule. Everyone on the selling team should have previous experience buying and selling companies. In addition, they should be very smart, quick, and good problem solvers. Problems are likely to arise both before starting and during the selling process; it will be very important to solve them quickly in order not to raise unnecessary questions, get bogged down, and disrupt the process.

  When you sell your company, your team will be up against a team of experts who negotiate the buying and selling of companies constantly, and they know how to do it, including the preparation of the final documents memorializing the sale. These must be done carefully to minimize potential future financial exposure and legal problems.

- **Manage your investment bankers**

  It's a good idea to begin talking to investment bankers early. Don't wait until you're finally ready to sell. Get acquainted with them. Check out your chemistry, their knowledge about selling companies, and their relevant market experience.

  This is a perfectly acceptable practice, and you can explain to them that if you are ever in a situation of wanting to sell in the future, you want to be in a good position to make a well-informed selection. By doing this, you will learn a great deal about the process of selling companies, and you will learn about the individual bankers' advantages and disadvantages.

Soon after making the decision to sell, you should lay the foundation for a "bake-off" among the investment bankers. You and your lead director should visit your selections from your initial "get acquainted" meetings and from your industry contacts at their offices. These meetings will help you select the two or three finalists who will be invited to make a presentation to your entire board of directors. Set up a schedule for the finalists to come to a conference room at your bank, your law firm, your accounting firm, or your private club for a final presentation and interview. Confidentiality is very important, and that is the reason *not* to meet at your company.

Following the presentations, the selling CEO/family leader and the board of directors will gather to discuss attributes of the investment bankers and make a selection. The chosen banker will then meet with you and your CFO to make the plan to move forward. Information requests should go to the CFO, and all questions about the process should go to you as the leader of the selling process.

Investment bankers will want as much control of the process as possible, but it is imperative that you stay in the loop all the way through the process, up until the buyer wires the funds to your bank.

Sellers should never communicate directly with the buyers. All communications should go through the investment banker. On occasion, there may be a reason the investment banker wants you to meet with the buyer; the banker will organize the meeting and attend.

Investment bankers work for you, not the other way around. All investment bankers want as much control of the process as possible, but they are advisors, and you are the principal. Therefore, they cannot agree to anything or make any representations without you knowing about them in advance.

- **Establish criteria for selecting the buyer of your company**
If maximizing the price paid for your company is your primary objective, you should sell to a strategic buyer who will make

the decision based on their corporate strategy. Strategic buyers expect to get substantial leverage from acquisitions. Reasons for making specific acquisitions vary; so learning as much as you can about each potential buyer's objectives can help you position your company more advantageously.

Adding your company to one that would not have to increase their general and administrative costs but rather would be able to eliminate yours in the acquisition is a good example of efficiencies that can result.

If the products are similar, the buyer may see the opportunity to save marketing dollars. Therefore, making acquisitions that broaden the buyer's product line can be very synergistic.

Entry into new markets and gaining new customers can be a big benefit to acquirers. Then the acquiring company can buy more companies whose products are compatible with the one just purchased and disproportionately increase earnings because of elimination of redundant costs.

International companies may be looking for a business platform on which to build in another country.

There are many opportunities to disproportionately increase earnings through acquisitions, but in order for the sellers to realize maximum benefits, they must identify and understand the points of leverage and *actually make calculations to prove the benefits to the buyers.*

- **Have a backup plan—an alternative buyer**
  During the exploration period, it's an ideal time to examine a wide range of alternative opportunities to ultimately sell the stock of your company. Consult your attorneys and accountants about tax-advantaged plans to sell your stock or a portion of your stock to employees of the company. This, however, will be among the least lucrative exits. But it will establish a floor for the pricing of your company.

  Sales to private equity firms will yield a higher price than selling to employees but less than selling to a purely strategic buyer, unless the buyer is pursuing a strategic industry roll up. Then prices paid can be higher.

It will be smart to meet with a few private equity firms to learn about the criteria for their investments and the formulas they use for structuring deals and what you can expect to receive if you sell to them.

You will also be able to find out if they structure their deals so management can participate, the amount of ownership they will provide, and the terms of management's participation in the equity. This will give you an idea of private equity/venture capital firms' appetite for making acquisitions such as yours. The conversations should be preliminary and exploratory in nature.

Making contacts with these people to discuss your company and its future, while evaluating the possibilities of selling, before making any decisions, will provide great insight that will help your decision making. Not only that, but once you have selected a buyer, if the process breaks down, you will have a place to go in order to ramp up an alternative buyer.

- **Conduct due diligence on every prospective buyer before soliciting interest or sending an offering memorandum**
  If nothing else, get a complete credit report on the prospective buyers before spending time and effort cultivating them. Make sure they have adequate financial resources to do a deal.

  It's also a good idea to interview customers, dealers and retailers, distributors, and independent reps to learn about their reputation in the market. If you know of anyone who sold their company to them, interview them to see if they had a good experience selling to that particular buyer.

  Knowledge is power, and doing this kind of background checking and due diligence will strengthen your position or inform you that the people in the company are not those with whom you would want to do business.

- **Tailor your company story to demonstrate the best fit with each potential buyer**
  Before allowing your investment banker to reach out to any prospective buyer, do as much research as you can. Review their website, customer reviews, product literature, and any other

information you can gather. If possible, interview some people at the companies in their supply chain.

This background will make it possible for you to tailor your presentation to the company, and describe benefits for them to acquire your company. Look at both opportunities to increase revenue and to eliminate redundant costs.

- **If the buyer's desire to acquire your company is greater than your desire to sell to that buyer, you will be able to control the closing process**

The better job you are able to do in tailoring your company story to maximize the potential benefits for the acquirer, the more compelling buying your company will be.

The stronger the story, the more appeal there will be among potential acquirers. The greater the interest in your company appears to be, and the longer the list of revenue generation opportunities as well as overall cost-cutting opportunities, the more appeal you will have as an acquisition target. This will give you more power in the closing process.

If due diligence is dragging on, and if the closing date continues to be pushed back from the previously agreed upon closing date, you can quietly test the interest level with "backup buyers." And if there is interest, impose a final closing date, informing the people who are delaying that if they don't meet the new deadline, you will be selling to someone else, either employees or a private equity firm who is doing a deal with your management team. This approach requires finesse but is extraordinarily effective in getting the sale closed on a timelier basis.

- **Have an unbiased coach**

One of the best additions to your selling team is an unbiased coach who has previously gone through the process to be at your side or available to you 24-7 to help you get through the periods of high anxiety. An experienced coach will help you debunk representations by your investment banker or the buyer and will help you shape your responses to things that don't sound right to you.

AFTERWORD: TWENTY YEARS LATER

Our Company

At the beginning of the twenty-first century, the print publishing industry began its collapse. Online delivery of information would take over, and many magazines and newspapers failed. My prescient thoughts ten years earlier about the Internet and the damage it would bring to the economics of print publishing ultimately turned out to be true as the aggregate value of all companies in the publishing industry began a steep decline.

I stayed at my former company for all of six minutes after the wire transfer landed at my bank in Milwaukee from the buyer, PTN Publishing. Stanley Sills, the former president of ITT Publishing under the famous ITT CEO Harold Geneen, had acquired PTN in 1987 with the backing of Chase Venture Partners and Golder, Thoma, Cressey, Rauner. But the company was languishing, and the private equity partners were becoming impatient. By the year of my sale, 1994, seven years had passed since making their investment in PTN, and it was going nowhere.

PTN desperately needed to make a significant acquisition. They stepped up and made the best offer I received. Our company was smaller than PTN in terms of revenue but more profitable. It bulked up their company, and increased their earnings. The investors saw an exit. And I was happy with the deal.

I had gotten to know Sills earlier, at our trade association meetings. He was a loner, with a dour personality, but he had a great wife—smart and attractive with a warm personality. I actually enjoyed Stan's company, and if I hadn't befriended him, I think he would have been sitting alone in a corner. I had read a lot about his former boss, the legendary Harold Geneen, and was fascinated to hear Sills tell me stories about the tough CEO, who had monthly management meetings with 120 managers reporting on the performances of their businesses. Geneen thought nothing of dressing down managers in front of everyone if their performance wasn't stellar and, in some cases, even publicly firing them on the spot.

Sills wanted to meet our customers as part of his due diligence because we didn't have contracts with them. Why didn't we? Because we had mutual trust with our customers, we confirmed our deals with handshakes for many years. So instead of letting Sills contact our customers, I shared at length with him my philosophy and practice of "customers for life." Briefly, I believed, and our business proved, that it was better not to have to renew contracts every year but rather to treat our clients as customers for life by working to achieve partnership relationships. I told Sills that when he owned the company, he could meet his customers and make whatever rules he wanted.

I also knew that I didn't want this "Geneen-trained" CEO to meet our employees *before* he owned the company. How right I was! At his first meeting with all of our key employees after buying our company, he spent nearly forty-five minutes telling them that there was a new sheriff in town—that I was weak and he was tough—and life would be different. This speech triggered an exodus of key people from our company. Many started new companies—some of which were competitors.

Immediately after closing the sale of our company, Sills—at the direction of his investors—began looking for exits. He and his partners had paid approximately twenty times after tax earnings for our company—$25 million. It was a lower multiple for PTN after they stripped the company of our generous profit-sharing program and numerous other employee benefits and events. They also eliminated new product development expenses and ceased all start-ups that were in the works. He slashed travel expenses and eliminated company aircraft in spite of the effective way they were used. It was ironic after Sills pulled the plug on one new publication that was being launched; he threatened to sue the team that had been working on it at our company when they left to do it on their own. Using our start-up formula, the new magazine quickly became profitable, and the company was sold within a few years for several million dollars.

Few acquirers were interested in buying PTN, and there was little traction, although Prudential Insurance Company offered $120 million, which was $30 million short of what Sills and his partners thought the company was worth.

Then, three years after PTN bought our company, two former executives of Turner Broadcasting, Gerry Hogan and Blair Schmidt-Fellner, met with Sills at PTN headquarters in Long Island, New York. Hogan and Schmidt-Fellner decided to pass on the opportunity after talking to

Sills. However, after telling him of their decision, Gerry Hogan decided, based on a quirky intuition, to make a trip to Fort Atkinson, Wisconsin, to see the former Johnson Hill Press and meet some of the people.

Upon leaving the building of Johnson Hill Press, Hogan called Schmidt-Fellner and told him to call the venture backers of PTN to tell them they would be willing to acquire the company for $97 million. And Hogan directed Schmidt-Fellner to set up a meeting in Chicago with the venture partners that would not include Sills. Why this drastic turnabout? Hogan had found the secret sauce: a series of protocols, procedures, and processes for creating magazines that had targeted local, regional, national, and international reach, including various means for creating and nurturing customers for life, along with a series of talented publishers personally trained by me. Hogan and Schmidt-Fellner bought the company not for the physical magazines but for the intellectual property that lay behind them. These processes could be applied to all their other holdings. The deal was done in short order.

It was thus logical that Hogan and Schmidt-Fellner made the decision to do exactly the opposite of PTN. They decided to shift the headquarters to Wisconsin and merge the PTN business and culture into the Johnson Hill Press organization. The company became Cygnus Business Media.

The Cygnus owners made several divestitures and a like number of strategically beneficial acquisitions; and even though they were not interested in selling, they received an unsolicited offer for $275 million in mid-2000 from Paul Mackler, a former publishing industry executive, and a private investment backer, ABRY Partners, LLP.

Four years later, in 2009, after a spending spree and a parade of new CEOs, ABRY was preparing to walk away from Cygnus, leaving the keys to the company on GE Capital's desk. They were the largest of a syndicate of twenty-three lenders.

Following bankruptcy and a financial restructuring wiping out $180 million of debt, the company was recapitalized at $60 million, and GE Capital was the sole owner. John French was brought in by GE to determine how to exit the Cygnus investment. He did a brilliant job restructuring the company and selling off publishing assets in five different sales that generated more than the $60 million debt GE was holding.

French accomplished this in five years, and most of the employees stayed with the new buyers and did not have to move. It was a remarkable feat.

In this situation, the whole was not greater than the sum of its parts—rather, the sum of its parts was greater than the whole.

I sold to PTN in 1994; PTN sold to Cygnus Business Media in 1997; Cygnus sold to Paul Mackler and ABRY Partners in 2000; GE took over the bankrupt company in 2009 and hired John French to liquidate it. He sold the five divisions to individual buyers, completing the last of the sales in 2014, exactly twenty years after I sold to PTN. Many of the employees who didn't leave the company survived five different owners after our family sold plus went through a bankruptcy.

Personal Reflections

Since I was a little boy, I loved business. (I was a business child.) Even more, I loved talking with people about business. I was a hands-on CEO/ owner, involved in the development of our company through launching magazines. During one month, about a year and a half before selling, I was in thirty cities and in twenty-two states in nineteen days. Over twenty-seven years of ownership, with a few respites, that was my schedule, although not always as extreme. Fortunately, we effectively used our airplanes for developing our company as we did; otherwise our reach and timing would have been impossible. Many towns were lucky to have an airstrip, let alone an airport.

After staying in small motels in sometimes dusty, dingy midwestern towns, with their empty, vacant main streets, I was tired and losing passion for the business. Most significantly, I had no heirs interested in taking the company to the third generation, and maybe most importantly, when I found out what my company would bring in a sale, I knew *there was no euphoria I could ever enjoy if I received more that would offset the despair I would feel if I received less.* Even when the company was sold for the third time for $275 million, I didn't have a nanosecond of regret for selling when I did.

I had set up trusts for my family members, creating financial security for four generations of our business family—my grandchildren,

children, both sets of parents, and my wife and me. We were all secure, and I was happy with the financial outcome.

A few months after selling, the euphoria began to feel like being on a very loose pulley, as a make-believe businessman renting and equipping an outside office, considering various investments. I also built a home office suite and hired a private butler to serve at breakfast, luncheon, and dinner "business meetings" that I hosted at my home along with my new business partner.

To my surprise my wife's schedule was jam-packed with volunteer meetings and boards, mountain-climbing expeditions, taking art classes, painting, and training to be a Pilates instructor. She had, basically, no time for me. Our beautiful house on Lake Drive in Milwaukee had so many lovely venues for long breakfasts, lunches, and dinners and long conversations. My new butler was an Italian trained chef. But my wife had created her own full-time life. And it didn't include leisurely conversations with me—not surprising given my previous intense travel and work schedule and four years living in Switzerland.

My wife and I did continue our international travel with the Young Presidents' Organization (YPO). (I have visited most countries in the world two or three times.) During one of these adventures, I had a very fortuitous encounter that would, in retrospect, change the very course of my life.

While going through customs in Zimbabwe in early 1995, I saw John Davis standing in line. Years earlier, as a PhD student, he had written a Harvard Business School case study about generational transition, using the story about my father, my brother, and me.

Although it is still used at Harvard today, I had not seen John for many years before our African encounter. In the interim, John had been a founding faculty member at the Leading the Family Business program at IMD—a famous international business school in Lausanne, Switzerland.

During our visit, he suggested that he recommend me to the school to be an executive-in-residence. I wasn't really sure what that was, but it sounded appealing, and thus several conversations began over the week when he helped me map out the next phase of my life's journey.

My wife and daughter encouraged me to pursue the opportunity. My wife, however, had a caveat. I had named the tune in our lives to date. Now she had her own life as a prominent philanthropist in our community, and she did not want to give that up.

While our original plan had been to be in Switzerland for a year, it turned into four when several faculty members recommended that I pursue a doctorate at Business School Lausanne. I loved teaching and had received high evaluations from the international body of graduate students from thirty countries. My wife encouraged me to go for it.

My fascination with entrepreneurship and its intersect with the study of family business influenced me to join a doctoral program in Switzerland and begin the research underlying this book. After defending my dissertation and passing my exams, I became a professor of entrepreneurship at the University of Wisconsin–Madison School of Business, continued my research, and began an advisory practice on selling owner-managed and family companies.

The blend of academic study with my applied experience provided a unique perspective among faculty members and gave me a powerful jump-start in studying the mosaic of founder and controlling owner-managed companies, multishareholder family companies, and related issues of responsible stewardship. My studies and academic research fueled the respect I had for the mentors I was fortunate to have during my career.

I have been blessed with an abundance of learning opportunities provided by the corporate boards on which I served, consulting assignments, faculty colleagues, and my students in the Families in Business program at the Harvard Business School, IMD, and the University of Wisconsin–Madison School of Business. My students' boundless curiosity has inspired my personal commitment to lifelong learning. My colleagues at the Cambridge Family Enterprise Group have amplified my knowledge and insight into family-owned businesses and business families. I have tremendous gratitude for everything they've given me.

When I returned to the States, with my newly minted credentials and my faculty appointment at the University of Wisconsin, teaching undergraduates and graduate students in addition to the Executive MBA capstone course, I was energized by my new career. I had just defended my dissertation: "Toward a Model for Making and Executing the Decision to Sell: An Exploratory Study of the Sale of Family Owned Companies." I had become a regular visiting lecturer at the Families in Business executive program at Harvard Business School where I spoke about succession and generational transfer, business governance (outside boards of directors), and selling the family business.

Returning home with a doctorate on top of a successful business career and service on many boards, the invitations to become involved in other activities were nearly endless. When I realized how thinly I was being stretched, I put all of my obligations on a spreadsheet and realized I had accepted commitments for more days than there are in a year. For sure, I was on an ego trip feeling wanted and in demand. But yikes, I had given up my life.

But not only was I too busy, I also wasn't happy. I had too many commitments; I didn't like the political infighting among faculty at the university, and I knew my wife and I were going through the motions while living parallel lives. The first year we lived in Lausanne, my wife was there a little less than half time. The second year, it was a quarter of her time. The third, she made two cameo appearances in Europe and didn't come to Switzerland at all in the fourth. Needless to say, we were clearly on separate paths.

Finally, I wondered why. Who were we staying together for? It didn't seem like we were doing it for ourselves. Our daughter was thirty-two, and our son was thirty. Frankly, to stay together for them didn't seem authentic. After all, we had been effectively separated for four years, and we were both happier then. When I was living in Switzerland and my wife in Milwaukee, we didn't have to deal with the reality we were both facing—until, that is, I returned.

We talked about separating and ultimately decided to get divorced. It wouldn't be overly complicated because virtually all of our assets were liquid, and I had no qualms about her getting one half of our assets in a divorce. I was grateful for the wife and mother she was in our thirty-five years of marriage. Unfortunately, I handled our separation and ultimate divorce in a ham-handed way, and that's putting it nicely. The truth is, I was insensitive, lacked empathy, and was dishonest.

Reality flared up, and I had an appointment with a prominent psychiatrist from India, Dr. Ashok Bedi, who was conjoining spiritual principles with Jungian analysis in his practice. I shared something I had written in Switzerland:

> *You can change the externals in your life and things will be okay for a while. But to get profound change you have to look at yourself. It's hard to get from the point where you are in pain and can't stand it, to the point where your new reality emerges. It's not easy to come up with a new way of living your life that will work. Are you better off staying where you are—in pain but with some comfort and control—or try something that looks like it will be better but later realizing that nothing is as good as it seems at a distance.*

While I took many journeys and traveled incessantly during my working years, there was no journey as long or as hard as the journey I had to make from my head to my heart. And this is the shift that must come at this later stage of life—what I happily call "the glide path." I had to learn that rather than looking outside myself for meaning and acceptance and valorization, I needed to look within, for that is where my real and true strength and happiness lie. And for this, I needed to tame my outsized ego and befriend and quiet my sometimes cascading, ruminating thoughts.

My highest goals became contentment and joy—and the ability to lean into whatever pain comes my way. I am learning the power of the pause, the beauty of restraint of reactions, and the healthy simplicity of a smile in a tense moment. I believe there is a greater power in the universe than my ego. However, I admit that sometimes I still marvel at what I accomplished from a small farming community in Wisconsin.

My distinguished professor wife (an older, not a younger woman, by the way) captured my attention and my heart. And because of things that happened in her life, she was able to guide me in my effort to seek a spiritual path in the past sixteen years. She was a single mom for twenty-five years and is a feminist; I was a CEO—a business owner with some narcissistic and chauvinistic characteristics that I did not want to have. We both had shrinks on speed dial, learning so much in the process.

I had written a letter to myself on New Year's Day in 2001. I no longer wanted to chase materialism. Rather I wanted to find contentment and equanimity. And I was going to have to work hard because those things were not in my DNA. When anyone mentioned his or her soul, I just felt a hollow tube within.

When I first encountered her in the hospital coffee shop, I was smitten. And shortly thereafter our journey together began. She has been a teacher, a coach, traveling companion, and a true soul mate—the type of person I always wanted in my life but never found.

We retired from teaching together and moved to California in 2002, leaving Milwaukee and my circle of friends to my ex-wife. With the help of John Davis and Distinguished Professor Emerita Patricia Mellencamp, I have finally completed this book that has been in the works since completing my doctorate seventeen years ago. I can finally admit I have been engulfed in fear for all this time that what I know or what I write just isn't good enough. I don't feel that way anymore.

A MODEL FOR MAKING AND EXECUTING THE DECISION TO SELL FAMILY OWNED COMPANIES

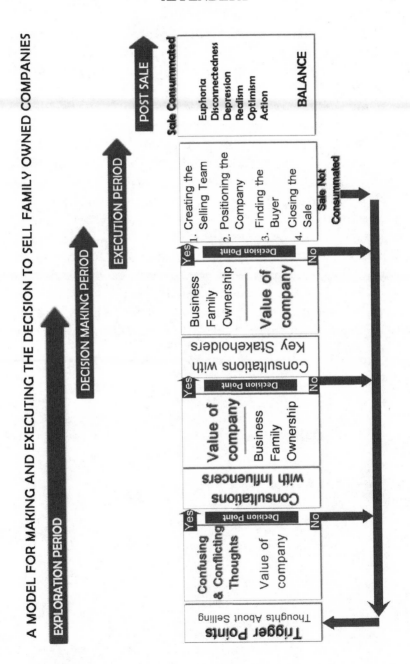

This diagram illustrates the periods and process of exploring, making the decision, and selling a family company. If this company is to be sold, the decision to sell will be reached during the exploration period, depicted with an arrow at the top of the model. When an affirmative decision is made to sell the company, it's difficult, if not impossible, to pinpoint the exact time it happens. As more and more information is gathered during the exploration period, ultimately if the decision to sell is going to be reached, it just happens when the information gathered makes a compelling case for selling. After the decision is made to sell, the execution period kicks in. After the selling and closing process is successfully completed, the postsale period begins.

The chart illustrates the repetitive cycle of gathering more and more information—divided among business issues, family considerations, and ownership desires, for example, to sell or not. The fair market value of the company and division or product line to be sold are critically important parts of the ownership considerations. After each cycle of consideration, a definitive decision is made to sell or not. The decision not to sell requires a recommitment to company ownership. An effective process requires thorough analysis of business issues, family considerations, and the impact on ownership at each stage.

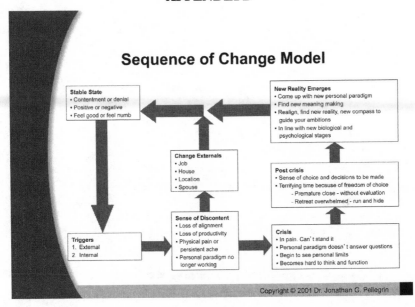

Sequence of Change Model

Stable State
- Contentment or denial
- Positive or negative
- Feel good or feel numb

New Reality Emerges
- Come up with new personal paradigm
- Find new meaning making
- Realign, find new reality, new compass to guide your ambitions
- In line with new biological and psychological stages

Change Externals
- Job
- House
- Location
- Spouse

Post crisis
- Sense of choice and decisions to be made
- Terrifying time because of freedom of choice
  - Premature close - without evaluation
  - Retreat overwhelmed - run and hide

Sense of Discontent
- Loss of alignment
- Loss of productivity
- Physical pain or persistent ache
- Personal paradigm no longer working

Triggers
1. External
2. Internal

Crisis
- In pain. Can't stand it
- Personal paradigm doesn't answer questions
- Begin to see personal limits
- Becomes hard to think and function

This model illustrates psychological and emotional factors that come into play when making decisions about significant life changes. Going through a *sense of discontent* and simply changing the externals—like your job, your house, where you live, and your spouse/partner—provide temporary relief, at best. Going through paralyzing crises in contemplating change can lead to deeper thinking, finding new reality that can lead you to making lasting and fulfilling change.

During consideration of selling a company, this chart can be useful in guiding family members and shareholders through a process that might end up making them comfortable with whatever decision is reached regarding ownership of the company.

ACKNOWLEDGMENTS

There are many people who touched my life in significant ways and helped to shape both my business and academic careers that finally led to this book. Dudley Godfrey (and his protégé, John Peterson), Bob Feitler, Harry Quadracci, Barry Allen, and Bill Gorman. Amazingly, I formed my board when my company was in trouble and I needed serious advice. They all agreed to serve, and their sobering advice and counsel were the keys to our turnaround and ultimate successful sale.

Jim Rosemurgy, my cousin and college roommate, has been my closest confidant throughout my life. He is the smartest and most business-savvy entrepreneur and company founder I have ever met. Jim built an exceptionally strong company headquartered in the competitive South Florida market. He is a brilliant financial architect and business leader and has not only engendered the utmost respect in both his industry and his community, but he also effectively passed the baton of leadership to his successor CEO ten years ago in addition to passing the entire ownership of his company to his three children. He is truly a remarkable example of a business family leader.

YPO (Young Presidents' Organization) broadened my world view immensely from my small town, rural background. I particularly appreciated the wise recommendations of my forum members, Dick Egan and Jack Jacobus. They were both there for me when others turned their back. Equally valuable was learning what not to do from the mistakes of others.

Lee Morris was a classmate at Harvard Business School's Owner/President Management Program and a fellow member of YPO. We have had a great impact on each other's careers. We have both been committed to lifelong learning and benefited greatly from applying the knowledge we gained as valued advisors to each other.

Publishing industry executives who were willing to take me under their wing when I was a young man jump-started my own accumulation of experience and knowledge. Those who were extraordinarily helpful in my career were John Suhler, Bob Edgell, Dick Moeller, Gerry Hobbs, Roger Friedman, Ken Nelson, and Bill Gorman. I am grateful for everything they shared with me.

The executives from whom I learned the most at Johnson Hill Press were Ernie Pope, Don Henning, John Stewart, Mike Murrell, Bob Lederer, Pat Nadler, Rich Reiff, Steve Davidson, and Jan Reck. While it wasn't always easy, I grew from what each of them taught me, and I am thankful they were in my life.

The following individuals shaped my life *after* the sale of our family company. From them I received the gift of an extraordinarily stimulating and productive chapter of the final years of my life. How can I ever thank them enough?

John Davis, whom I met in 1980 when he was a doctoral student at Harvard Business School, has done more than anyone else in guiding me through the period *after* I sold my company. He was incredibly helpful to me when I was a "later in life doctoral student," actively serving on my dissertation committee and providing immeasurable help on this book. I will be forever grateful for the rich dimension he has added to my life. Professor Davis founded the Families in Business: From Generation to Generation program at Harvard Business School in 1996 and continues to serve as its faculty chair. He teaches in the Owner/ President Management program as well as other HBS executive programs. In addition, he is the founder and chairman of the Cambridge Family Enterprise Group.

Alden Lank, professor emeritus of Organizational Behavior and chair of the Leading the Family Business program at IMD in Lausanne, Switzerland, invited me to be an executive in residence in 1996. Nine months later, Alli encouraged me to become a doctoral student and write my dissertation on the sale of family companies. He was a great mentor and advisor who introduced me to academia. His intellect, wisdom, and extraordinary teaching skills were inspirations to me.

Together with John Davis, John Ward was a member of the original faculty of family business scholars who founded the Leading the Family Business program at IMD in 1987. During my four years in Switzerland, Professor Ward served on my dissertation committee sharing his knowledge and wisdom along with Alli Lank and John Davis. I learned so much from these three leaders in the field as they guided me in my research on selling family businesses. John Ward is currently serving as clinical professor of Family Enterprise and codirector of the Center for Family Enterprises at Northwestern University's Kellogg School of Management. In addition, Professor Ward is a cofounder of the Family Business Consulting Group.

Susanne Hanson was my research assistant for three years. She put everything she had—her professionalism, tenacity, language skills, curiosity, organizational skills, and ability to relate to all different kinds of people—into researching and helping me write my doctoral dissertation. She worked tirelessly and gave me the boost I needed to complete this project at an advanced age. I owe her a debt of gratitude.

Robert Pricer, professor of Entrepreneurship and director of the Weinert Center for Entrepreneurship at the University of Wisconsin–Madison School of Business, invited me to speak to his MBA students before I completed my doctorate. That day, he began persuading the Business School dean, Andrew Policano, to extend an offer to me to join the faculty as Bob's colleague. Bob was an inspiring professor who taught me how to engage students who wanted to become entrepreneurs. I will be forever grateful to Bob for taking me under his wing as perhaps one of the oldest new faculty members ever. Three CEOs on whose boards I served provided me with stimulating opportunities. In addition, they became close personal friends–like family. Roger Dirksen, Tom Doerr and Peter Mahler.

My wife, Patricia Mellecamp, a distinguished professor emerita of film and media studies at the University of Wisconsin–Milwaukee, gave me the final push to write this book that I had been thinking about for many years. I am so grateful for her disciplined guidance, to say nothing of her experience editing four collections of essays and writing her own books and essays.

And finally, to my dad, George, who started not one but two successful family businesses—one that he turned over to me and another that he turned over to my brother. His willingness to pass the baton to the next generation before normal retirement age and make it possible for my brother, Dave, and me to own our respective companies was an act of extraordinary generosity for which we are both eternally grateful. He was an incredible, loving father.

Made in the USA
San Bernardino, CA
29 October 2018